UFO
ABDUCTIONS

UFO ABDUCTIONS

A DANGEROUS GAME

PHILIP J. KLASS

UPDATED EDITION

PROMETHEUS BOOKS
Buffalo, New York

This book is dedicated to those who will needlessly bear mental scars for the rest of their lives because of the foolish fantasies of a few.

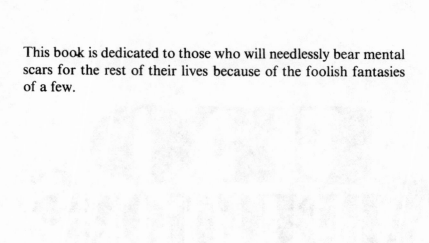

Library of Congress Card Catalog No. 87-43249
ISBN: 0-87975-509-1

Contents

Preface to Revised Edition

Perhaps you are one of the many tens of thousands who have read the best-selling book *Communion,* by Whitley Strieber, published in early 1987, which strongly suggests he was abducted by strange-looking creatures from UFOs and subjected to terrible indignities. Possibly you read the book *Intruders,* by Budd Hopkins, also published in early 1987, which suggests that hundreds of people have become victims of UFO-abduction as part of an extraterrestrial genetic experiment.

Probably you are one of many millions who have seen or heard Strieber and Hopkins describe these bizarre experiences on national or local television and radio talk-shows. Possibly you will be one of the millions who will see the movie *Communion,* based on Strieber's book, to be released in the spring of 1989.

Under the circumstances, it would be surprising if you were not at least curious whether such bizarre incidents are really happening. And it would be understandable if you wondered whether you or a member of your family might suffer such an encounter. Conceivably you may even suspect that you or a member of your family already has had such an experience.

Would you like to know the truth?

The public has been hoodwinked and brainwashed. After having spent more than 22 years investigating famous, seemingly mysterious UFO reports—including some of the earliest claims of UFO abduction—I can assure you that there is absolutely no scientifically credible physical evidence to indicate that the earth is being visited by extraterrestrials—let alone that they are abducting people.

How confident am I that "UFO-abductions" are fantasy? Confident enough to risk personal bankruptcy. I will pay $10,000 to each and every victim of UFO-abduction if that claim is confirmed by the Federal Bureau of Investigation—the national law enforcement agency responsible for crimes of kidnapping in the United States (as detailed in Chapter 16). I first made that offer publicly in the spring of 1987. To my knowledge, not one of the many recent UFO-abduction claimants has reported it to the FBI.

UFO-Abductions: A Dangerous Game is the story of how the relatively harmless UFO myth has become a dangerous cult. It is a cult that threatens the mental health, perhaps even the life, of those who unwittingly become participants.

Philip J. Klass

Washington D.C.
November 16, 1988

One

The UFO-Abduction Era Begins

It was the third week of September 1966, and the "UFO Era" was almost 20 years old, when the October 4 issue of *Look* magazine hit the stands with the story of Betty Hill and her husband, Barney, who claimed that they had been abducted by a UFO five years earlier and subjected to a superficial physical examination by curious but friendly UFOnauts. Many thousands of persons had reported seeing UFOs since they were first "discovered" in June 1947. And, despite the lack of any credible, physical evidence and repeated U.S. Air Force disclaimers, some people suspected that UFOs might be extraterrestrial craft.

    Look magazine took a nearly full-page advertisement in the *New York Times* to promote the two-part series by John G. Fuller. The ad said in part: "On September 19, 1961, Betty and Barney Hill of Portsmouth, New Hampshire, 'sighted' a flying saucer. The experience shook them; worse, it left them with two 'lost' hours. Ultimately, they sought help from a distinguished Boston psychiatrist and neurologist. Under psychotherapy, including time-regression hypnosis, they both told extraordinary stories of being 'kidnapped' aboard an alien space vessel, and of interrogation and examination by 'humanoid' creatures. After seven months of treatment, the doctor decided that neither patient was psychotic, and both consciously and under hypnosis told what they believe to be absolute truth."

Barely a month later, on October 29, 1966, I interviewed Dr. Ben Simon, the experienced Boston psychiatrist who had treated the Hills. We met in Washington where he had come to attend a conference of the American Psychiatric Association. He had brought along tape recordings of some of the Hills' hypnosis sessions for use in a brief talk he planned to deliver.

Dr. Simon told me a most revealing story. He said that before *Look* had decided to publish the two articles on the Hills' tale, the magazine sent one of its top editors to Boston to talk with him. Dr. Simon said: "The first question he asked me was this: 'Doctor, do you really believe that the Hills were abducted and taken aboard a flying saucer?' " Dr. Simon said he replied: *"Absolutely not!"* Later in their discussion, the psychiatrist said, the senior *Look* editor told him: "Doctor, if you had replied to my first question by saying that you really believed that the Hills had been abducted, I would have put on my hat and taken the next flight back to New York."

Yet *Look* proceeded to publish the two articles, which served to promote Fuller's soon-to-follow book, *Interrupted Journey: Two Lost Hours Aboard a Flying Saucer*. The newsstand sales of these two issues (October 4 and 11) broke all previous records.

During our October 29 discussion, Dr. Simon told me that seven offers for movie rights to the Hills' story already had been received, "the lowest of which is $300,000." He added, "I'm not going to tell you the highest bid." (Under the terms of their contract, author Fuller and Dr. Simon each received 30 percent of the royalties from the *Look* articles, the Fuller book, and film rights, while the Hills received 40 percent. Later, when I was a guest in Dr. Simon's home, he told me of the heated debate among the principals over their respective shares of the proceeds.)

The UFO incident had occurred around midnight as the Hills were driving back from Montreal on Highway 3, which winds through the White Mountains of New Hampshire, en route to their home in Portsmouth. Somewhere south of Lancaster, Betty, who already "believed" in UFOs according to her husband, decided that they were being followed by a bright starlike object.

When Barney finally stopped the car and got out for a better view, he became frightened and jumped back into the car, expressing the fear that they might be captured by the UFO. If a UFO was indeed following them as they drove along Highway 3, as both now suspected, it would be logical to divert to a less conspicuous road. (Later, Betty would recall that they had turned off onto Highway 175, and later onto an obscure side road. Perhaps they had even pulled off the road in the hope that they could shake the UFO.)

Considering these diversions and time spent later trying to find their way back to the main highway, it is not surprising that they arrived back in Portsmouth roughly two hours later than originally expected.

The next morning Betty promptly called her sister Janet, who also was interested in UFOs, to tell her of the previous night's exciting experience. Her sister suggested that Betty and Barney might have been "irradiated" by the UFO and said she would check with a neighbor who was a physicist. According to Betty, Janet called back shortly to say that an ordinary magnetic compass could be used to check for radiation—which simply is not correct.

Betty found a compass, brought it near their car, and noted that its needle began to behave erratically (due to the ferrous metal in the car's body). As a result, according to Fuller's book, "Betty was haunted by the thought that they might have been exposed to radioactivity." This prompted her to go to the local library and take out the book *The Flying Saucer Conspiracy,* by Donald Keyhoe, director of the National Investigations Committee on Aerial Phenomena (NICAP), then the nation's largest group of "UFO-believers." She read it in one sitting.

On September 26, 1961, less than one week after the Hills' adventure, Betty sat down and wrote to NICAP's director, describing their UFO sighting. *But she did not mention a possible abduction.*

Several days afterward, Betty had a nightmare in which she *dreamed* that she and Barney had been abducted and taken aboard a flying saucer. She had the same nightmare for the next four nights. Betty recounted her UFO-abduction story to friends and fellow social workers as nothing more than a recurring dream, until her supervisor suggested that perhaps it was more than that. One of her coworkers suggested that Betty write down the details of her nightmares, which she did.

When NICAP received Betty's letter, it asked one of its New England members, Walter Webb, to interview the Hills, which he did on October 21. The following month, two more NICAP investigators—C. D. Jackson and Robert Hohman—spent 12 hours with the Hills, and during this time Betty told them of her abduction nightmares. When Jackson and Hohman learned that the Hills arrived back in Portsmouth around 5:00 A.M., about two hours later than originally expected, they asked why it had taken so long; and they raised the possibility that, if Betty's nightmares were based on reality, this could explain the two hours of "missing time." This was the genesis of the idea that "missing time" is the fingerprint of UFO-abductions, which later emerged as the gospel according to many UFOlogists.

In mid-1962, Barney's physician, who had treated him for ulcers and high blood pressure, recommended he see a psychiatrist, Dr. Duncan Stephens, of Exeter, New Hampshire. Stephens concluded that at least some of Barney's problems might stem from feelings of guilt over having left his black wife and children (Barney was black) to marry a white woman (Betty). He recommended that Barney visit Dr. Simon, a prominent Boston psychiatrist who had acquired considerable skill in the use of regressive-hypnosis for treating certain psychiatric problems. By this time, Betty was giving lectures to local groups, describing the UFO incident and her abduction dreams.

Betty accompanied Barney on his first visit to Dr. Simon's office on December 14, 1963. The psychiatrist told me he was surprised when Betty followed her husband into the doctor's consulting room, but added that it quickly became apparent that she too could benefit from treatment.

Using regressive hypnosis, Dr. Simon explored problems arising out of their interracial marriage in a small New England town as well as seeking details of their UFO encounter. It soon became clear to Dr. Simon that the Hills had indeed seen a bright starlike UFO and had been very frightened because they thought it was following them.

But the experienced psychiatrist quickly recognized that the abduction tale was only fantasy. One of the first clues, Dr. Simon told me, was that *both* Betty and Barney, under hypnosis administered separately, recalled in similar detail the events that had occurred during the drive down from Montreal, as would be expected for a shared experience. But this was *not* true for the alleged abduction.

Under regressive hypnosis, which was used as a memory aid, Betty recalled many details of the alleged abduction while Barney could recall very few. This, Dr. Simon emphasized, showed that the alleged abduction was *not* a shared experience. The psychiatrist was at first puzzled over how Barney had acquired even a few details of the incident. But he learned that Betty enjoyed recounting her abduction dreams to friends, neighbors, and UFO investigators and that Barney often was present on those occasions, sometimes reading the newspaper or watching television.

When Dr. Simon played tape recordings of Barney reliving the experience of stopping the car to get out for a closer look at the UFO, one could easily detect the terror in Barney's voice as he screamed for help. Dr. Simon told me he had never had a patient become so violent, and I could hear the psychiatrist's voice on the tape reassuring Barney that the UFO could not harm him.

But when Dr. Simon played the recording of Betty reliving under regressive hypnosis what should have been the terrifying experience of being taken aboard an alien craft—not knowing if she and Barney might be dissected like frogs—her voice was as calm as if she were describing a trip to the local supermarket.

When Dr. Simon learned of the nightmares Betty had had two years earlier, and that she had written down the details at the time, he asked her to bring the notes into his office. When she did, he found that the tale she told under regressive hypnosis was essentially identical to her nightmare dreams.

When I asked Dr. Simon how he could be sure that the original nightmares were not themselves based on an actual experience, he pointed out a few of the many irrational inconsistencies of the abduction story. He stressed that such inconsistencies are characteristic of dreams.

For example, while Betty dreamed that the extraterrestrials spoke to her in English with a slight foreign accent, Barney recalled under hypnosis that they had no mouths. According to Betty's story, the ETs were familiar enough with earthly gadgets to know how to operate the zipper on her dress. But they were completely baffled by the fact that Barney's teeth could be removed, while Betty's were firmly anchored. Betty said she tried to explain to one of the spacemen that when some people get older they need artificial teeth, but he could not comprehend what was meant by age or the passage of time. Yet later, Betty said, when she was about to leave the flying saucer, the same spaceman said to her, "Wait a minute."

An important clue to the identity of the UFO that seemed to follow the Hills for many minutes came from Betty's description of the object under regressive hypnosis. She recalled seeing the nearly full moon and what she referred to as "a star down below the moon, on the lower left side of the moon. And then right after we left Lancaster, I noticed that there was a star, a bigger star up over this one [to the lower left of the moon]. And it hadn't been there before. And I showed Barney, and we kept watching it. It seemed to keep getting brighter and bigger looking."

Robert Sheaffer, a rigorous and skeptical UFO investigator who has been trained in astronomy, checked and found that Betty's recollections under hypnosis were correct for the night of the UFO incident. Just below and to the left of the moon, as Betty recalled, there was a starlike object—the planet Saturn. And just above Saturn, where Betty had described seeing a very bright starlike UFO, there was an exceptionally bright planet Jupiter. Because Betty did not describe seeing the moon, two nearby bright stars, *plus* a UFO, almost certainly the UFO that the Hills were observing at that time was an extremely bright planet Jupiter.

If you find it difficult to believe that the Hills could mistake a bright planet for a UFO that seemed to be following them, let me assure you that I too would have doubted such an explanation before I began investigating UFO cases more than 21 years ago. Experience—both mine and that of many others—has shown that most long-duration night-time UFO sightings turn out to be bright celestial bodies.

In 1973, the Center for UFO Studies (CUFOS) was created by the late Dr. J. Allen Hynek, a onetime UFO-skeptic and consultant to the U.S. Air Force for UFO investigations, who later became the spiritual leader of the UFO movement. CUFOS hired Allan Hendry as a full-time UFO investigator, and he later wrote a book reporting the results of his investigations: *The UFO Handbook* (1979).

Hendry reported that 28 percent of *all* UFOs reported to CUFOS during a 15-month period turned out to be bright celestial objects. In some cases, witnesses reported that these UFOs seemed to dart up and down, to wiggle, to swing like a pendulum, and, in one case, to ascend and descend.

During World War II, the crews of B-29s flying from the Mariana Islands to bomb Japan reported they were being followed by what was thought to be an enemy aircraft equipped with a powerful searchlight to enable enemy fighters to locate the bombers. For several weeks B-29 gunners tried, unsuccessfully, to shoot down the "searchlight plane" that seemed to be following them—until it was discovered that the object was a very bright planet Venus.

Still another case involving a USAF fighter trying to intercept a high-flying UFO at night was investigated by Hynek. His conclusion: "It seems certain that our harried pilot was pursuing [the star]

Capella." I myself, while driving at night on a four-lane highway, have observed Mars *seem* to follow me and to change its relative position. This resulted from the gently changing direction of the highway, which is not obvious to a driver in darkness.

A year before the two *Look* articles were published, a Boston newspaper carried a series of articles on the Hills' alleged UFO-abduction. Betty described the aftermath of this first publicity in a letter to her mother: "Public reaction was instantaneous—everyone wanted to know about our experience. We received telephone calls from Europe, Canada, and all over the United States; we were contacted by TV and radio stations; newspaper reporters visited; and letters—from everywhere. . . ."

While some of these letters came from people who reported their own UFO sightings, there was none from anyone who claimed also to have been an abduction victim—at least so far as Betty's letter indicates.

The impact of the *Look* articles a year later must have been far greater than that of the Boston newspaper series, considering the multimillion circulation the magazine then enjoyed. But if anyone wrote or called Betty Hill to claim they too were UFO-abduction victims, she did not disclose it at the time. (Many years later, a number of others would claim that they had had similar experiences prior to the Hills', but had not seen fit to "go public" with the story.)

NICAP director Keyhoe accepted the Hills' story of being followed by a UFO, but he declined to endorse the abduction story. It was too reminiscent of wild tales told a decade earlier by "contactees"—people who claimed to have made contact with UFOnauts and to have been given rides aboard their flying saucers. "Serious UFOlogists" like Keyhoe believed that the tales of contactees could only discredit the UFO movement. Even as late as 1973, when Keyhoe's book *Aliens From Space* was published, NICAP's director endorsed the findings of Dr. Simon, noting that the "supposed abduction was a psychological reaction."

Shortly after the Hill case achieved international fame, the

University of Colorado received a U.S. Air Force contract to conduct an independent study of UFOs. Early in the Colorado effort, the project sought recommendations from officials of NICAP and the Aerial Phenomena Research Organization (APRO), then the nation's oldest UFO organization, as to which cases it should investigate. Neither group recommended that Colorado University investigate the Hills' claim of abduction.

Dr. Edward U. Condon, who directed the Colorado study, later was criticized by some pro-UFOlogists for wasting his time in talking to several contactees and a person who had emerged in the wake of the *Look* articles to claim he too had been abducted by a UFO.

On July 29, 1968, Congressman J. Edward Roush, who was very much interested in UFOs, convened a one-day "UFO Symposium," at which five of the six scientists invited to appear were strongly pro-UFO. But not a single one of them mentioned the Hill case.

Yet within five years such abduction stories would begin to gain acceptance by "serious UFOlogists," and by the mid-1980s—as the UFO Era was starting its fifth decade—they would become the mainstream of the UFO movement, endorsed and embraced by many of its leaders.

Two

More Abductions, the Hill Star-Map

In 1967, the year after Betty and Barney Hill burst onto the public's awareness, Dr. Leo Sprinkle, a psychologist at the University of Wyoming, had his first experience using regressive hypnosis with a "near-abductee," whom he identifies only as a factory worker. The man alleged that a flying saucer had hovered over his car and tried, unsuccessfully, to coax him aboard.

Sprinkle, who characterizes himself as a "UFO-believer" as a result of his own two sightings, was a consultant to APRO and had recently launched a five-year research effort to explore whether persons who had observed UFOs had gained "psychic powers" as a result. If so, Sprinkle hoped to use their psychic abilities to predict where the next rash of UFO sightings ("flap") would occur. This would make it possible for experienced investigators to be present to take photographs and gather data.

While Sprinkle has never reported any encouraging results from this research effort, it did lead him into the study of UFO-abductions using hypnosis, in which he became a pioneer. But as of mid-1968, when Sprinkle submitted a position paper for publication in the proceedings of Congressman Roush's UFO symposium, he would only go so far as to say that he was "interested in the possibility that reliable observations are being made by persons who claim to see UFO occupants and, in some unusual cases, experience 'mental communications' with these UFO occupants."

As late as 1972, when Allen Hynek published his first book on UFOs, he took a cautious stance on the Hill case. Hynek said that their recollection of being followed by a UFO during the drive home "fits the pattern." But he characterized the abduction story as "atypical," adding that "when and if other cases of hypnotic revelation of close encounters become available for study . . . we will be able to note whether they also form a pattern."

Hynek did not have to wait long. The next year, 1973, beginning in early fall, the United States was enveloped by a major UFO flap, with hundreds of sighting reports from around the nation. And on the night of October 11, Charles Hickson and his young friend Calvin Parker reported they had been abducted and taken aboard a flying saucer for a superficial physical examination. The two men had been fishing near downtown Pascagoula, Mississippi. Hickson described his alleged abductors as being about five feet tall, with gray wrinkled skin "like an elephant." He claimed that the UFOnauts did not walk but "floated" and that their ears and eyes were cone-shaped.

Hynek and Dr. James Harder, a civil engineering professor, longtime "UFO-believer," and APRO consultant, visited Pascagoula and interviewed Hickson and Parker. Although Hickson's description of his abductors was vastly different from Betty Hill's account, Hynek stated publicly: "There is no question in my mind that these two men have had a very terrifying experience."

Harder offered an even stronger endorsement: "There was definitely something here that was not terrestrial. . . . Where they come from and why they were here is a matter of conjecture, but the fact that they are here is true, beyond a reasonable doubt."

With such strong endorsements from two "leading UFO experts," not only were Hickson and Parker featured on television network newscasts, but one or both of them also appeared on major television network talk-shows, including one hosted by Dick Cavett, which then had a large audience. Cavett introduced Hickson by reporting that he had just successfully passed a "lie detector" test, supporting his abduction story.

My own investigation into the Pascagoula case indicated it was a hoax, and I characterized it as such for reasons detailed at length in my book *UFOs Explained* (1974). Neither of the principals, nor Hickson's lawyer, Joseph Colingo—who had been trying to sell the movie rights for their abduction story for $1 million—ever wrote or called to challenge my conclusion. (Hickson, it turned out, had been fired from his previous job for improperly obtaining money from persons who worked under his direction.)

My investigation showed that the lie-detector test that Colingo had arranged for Hickson to take had been administered by a young, inexperienced polygraph examiner who had not finished his training and who was employed by a friend of Hickson's lawyer. Young Parker had a "nervous breakdown" before his scheduled polygraph test and was hospitalized. A week later Parker miraculously recovered in time to appear on a national television talk-show, but he never got around to taking a lie-detector test.

(In the late summer of 1975, after publication of my book, a major UFO conference was scheduled to be held at Fort Smith, Arkansas. The conference organizer, William Pitts, invited Hickson to speak and offered to pay all his travel expenses if he would take a new lie-detector test to be given by a polygraph examiner employed by the Fort Smith police department. Hickson agreed, prompting Pitts to believe that my own conclusions were wrong, and so I also was invited to attend, which I did. Shortly before the conference and before Pitts mailed Hickson his airline tickets, he called Hickson again to reconfirm the new lie-detector test arrangements. It was not until *after* Hickson arrived in Fort Smith and had lunched with Pitts that Hickson revealed he had changed his mind about taking a new lie-detector test given by an experienced police examiner.)

Hynek subsequently acknowledged, in an interview published in the August 1976 issue of *UFO Magazine,* that he had "been building

toward a positive attitude for a number of years when John Fuller
. . . told me the fascinating story of Betty and Barney Hill." "My
thinking was altered completely when I was called in, along with
Dr. James Harder, . . . to interrogate two Mississippi fishermen . . .
who insist they were literally 'kidnapped' and forced to go aboard
a spacecraft, where they were subjected—just as in the case of the
Hills—to a physical examination. The tale told by these two rugged
shipyard workers held up under grueling cross-examination," Hynek
said.

In early 1975, the Hills' abduction story seemed to gain impressive
scientific support as the result of the painstaking efforts of an Ohio
schoolteacher named Marjorie Fish and a series of articles published
in the December 1974 issue of *Astronomy* magazine, read by amateur
astronomers. The series was entitled "The Zeta Reticula Incident,"
by Terrence Dickinson, then the magazine's chief editor.

In Betty Hill's dreams, and as she reported during one of her
regressive-hypnosis sessions with Dr. Simon, one of the "spacemen"
pulled a map out of the wall and invited her to look at it. As Betty
described the incident, "There were all these dots on it. And they
were scattered all over it. Some were little, just pin points. And
others were as big as a nickel. And there were lines, there were
on some of the dots, there were curved lines going from one dot
to another. And there was one big circle, and it had a lot of lines
coming from it. A lot of lines going to another circle quite close,
but not as big. And these were heavy lines. And I asked him what
they meant. And he said that the heavy lines were trade routes.
And then the other lines, the other lines, the solid lines were places
they went occasionally. And he said the broken lines were expedi-
tions."

Betty said that when she asked the spaceman to point out his
"home port" he replied by asking her, "Where are you on the map?"
When Betty explained she didn't know, she said, the spaceman
responded: "If you don't know where you are, then there isn't any
point of my telling you where I am from," and he rolled the map

back into the wall.

During Betty's treatment by Dr. Simon, she had volunteered to try to draw the star-map as she recalled it, and the psychiatrist gave her the post-hypnotic suggestion to do so. And so in 1964, more than two years after the alleged incident, she sketched her recollections of the star-map, which was reproduced in Fuller's book but was given scant mention in the text.

Following publication of the *Look* articles and the Fuller book, amateur astronomer Marjorie Fish began to wonder if the positions of the tiny dots and large circles on Betty's sketch might correspond to the locations of actual stars, which could substantiate the abduction story. In discussions with Betty Hill on August 4, 1969, Ms. Fish was told that the map Betty Hill had been shown by the spacemen had been a three-dimensional representation that Betty had viewed from a distance of about three feet.

Fish faced a monumental task, considering the billions of stars in our galaxy, so she decided to limit her search to some 1,000 known stars within a distance of 55 light-years of our own sun. (If ETs could travel at the speed of light, whose velocity of 186,000 miles a second is believed to be the maximum possible, a round-trip visit to Earth would take 110 years.) As a further constraint, Fish limited her search to stars whose characteristics are believed by some astronomers to be potentially conducive to having planets that might sustain intelligent life.

The Ohio schoolteacher painstakingly used beads suspended by threads to represent the location of promising candidate stars, which she would then view from different angles seeking a pattern that corresponded to the one shown on Betty Hill's sketch. Her meticulous work was carried out between mid-1968 and early 1973.

Finally, Fish concluded that she had found a match for 15 of the larger dots and circles on Betty's star-map, one of which was our own sun, which was located on one of the heavy-line "trade routes." If Fish was correct, the home-base for the Hills' ET abductors was a planet of Zeta 2 Reticuli, one of a pair of stars. But Fish was *unable* to find a match for the other 11 "nearby" stars, more than 40 percent of those shown on Betty Hill's sketch.

While Fish was engaged in her painstaking task, so was another amateur astronomer, Charles W. Atterberg, of Elgin, Illinois. He came up with an even closer match of the Hill star-map than did Fish—*but with quite a different set of stars,* as described by Robert Sheaffer in his book *The UFO Verdict.*

After reading the articles in *Astronomy* magazine, Carl Sagan, the noted astrophysicist, and Steven Soter, a graduate student at Cornell University, used a computer to plot more accurately than Fish could do with suspended beads the locations of the 15 stars she had selected. As Sagan and Soter reported in the July 1975 issue of *Astronomy,* based on the more accurate computer plot of the 15 Fish star positions there was "little similarity" to those on Betty Hill's sketch.

Although Sagan has long been active in scientific efforts to search for extraterrestrial life, he and Soter wrote that Fish's results demonstrate "only that if we set out to find a pattern correlation between two nearly random data sets by selecting at will certain elements from each and ignoring others, we will always be successful. The argument cannot serve even to suggest a verification of the Hill story. . . . *Those of us concerned with the possibility of extraterrestrial intelligence must take care to demand adequately rigorous standards of evidence.*"

One of the strongest proponents of the significance of the Hill star-map is nuclear physicist Stanton Friedman, who earned his livelihood for more than a decade as a UFO lecturer before recently returning to his original profession. On February 22, 1981, Friedman and I debated at Trinity University, in San Antonio, Texas, and Friedman strongly endorsed the validity of the Betty Hill star-map, as he had so frequently done in the past.

I challenged Friedman's claim that Betty Hill could possibly recall, even with the aid of hypnosis, and reproduce precisely the location of 26 stars she allegedly had seen more than two years earlier. Then to test this critical issue I proposed that we conduct an experiment in which Friedman would play the role of Betty Hill. I had prepared a sketch very similar to Betty Hill's. The only difference was that I had shifted the locations of a few of the stars a fraction of an inch on my 8″ × 10″ star-map.

I proposed to let Friedman study my star-map closely for 30 seconds—a longer time than Betty Hill had had by her account. Then Friedman would return my star-map and would try to accurately recreate its star positions on a piece of thin, semi-transparent paper. When he had finished, we could place it atop my star-map to see how accurately he had been able to remember and reproduce the original.

I reminded Friedman that he would have an important advantage over Betty Hill because he knew in advance that he would be asked to reproduce it, whereas Mrs. Hill had no such warning or incentive for careful study.

Friedman flatly refused to try the experiment unless he was placed under hypnosis by Dr. Simon and given the post-hypnotic suggestion to draw my star-map. Certainly Friedman knew the post-hypnotic suggestion used was to help Betty Hill recall details of an incident that allegedly had occurred more than two years before. When I pressed Friedman to participate in the test, he responded, "When you have Dr. Simon here, I would be delighted." Shortly afterward Friedman admitted that he knew Dr. Simon had died a month before.

While the publication of "The Zeta Reticuli Incident" in *Astronomy* magazine in late 1974 briefly seemed to provide an aura of scientific support for the Hill abduction story, it did not generate any interest in the American Astronomical Society—the prestigious organization of professional astronomers—whose members would be especially interested if the Betty Hill star-map had any possible validity.

But the real bombshell that would impact on public consciousness exploded on October 20, 1975, when NBC-TV showed a two-hour movie during prime time called "The UFO Incident," dramatically portraying the UFO abduction of Betty and Barney Hill. This movie—which would be repeated, again in prime time, on September 9, 1976—triggered many UFO-abduction reports, including one where the "victim" would be missing for nearly five days.

Three

Travis Walton—Eager Abductee

NBC-TV's prime-time movie "The UFO Incident," starring James Earl Jones in the role of Barney Hill and Estelle Parsons as Betty, first shown on October 20, 1975, was tastefully done. It conveyed some of the Hills' emotional problems that Dr. Simon had uncovered, which had resulted from their interracial marriage in a small New England town at a time when such marriages were less commonplace than they are today. It also provided useful details for those who later would claim that they too had been abducted.

Shortly after the show aired, a young North Dakota woman named Sandy Larson contacted a local UFOlogist to report that she, her boyfriend, and her young daughter had been victims of a UFO-abduction that she claimed had occurred two months earlier. Later, under hypnosis administered by Dr. Leo Sprinkle, Mrs. Larson described how she and her two companions had been "stripped naked and all parts of our bodies examined . . . even our heads were opened up and all parts of our brains looked at. . . . We were dissected like frogs." Yet several hours later, when the three "victims" returned home, they were none the worse for their alleged ordeal, and there were no physical scars to substantiate Mrs. Larson's tale.

Then on the evening of November 5, 1975, barely two weeks

after the NBC movie, six young woodcutters called Under-sheriff L. C. Ellison, in Heber, to report that they had been working in Sitgreaves National Forest, in east-central Arizona, and that another woodcutter, named Travis Walton, had been "zapped" by a hovering UFO. They told Ellison they had driven off in fright but then had mustered enough courage to return, only to find young Walton gone— seemingly a UFO-abduction victim.

Not until five days later did Travis reappear, a few miles from the site where he reportedly had been zapped, to tell a story of having been taken aboard a flying saucer and given a superficial physical examination. The case was unique in several respects. Not only was it the first in which the alleged abduction was reported to law-enforcement authorities while the "victim" was still missing, but it was the first in which there were six supporting witnesses. Three months later, on February 7, 1976, it was announced that Travis Walton and his older brother Duane had taken lie-detector tests, administered by polygraph examiner George J. Pfeifer, which they had passed.

Seemingly this was the best substantiated of all UFO-abduction stories to date. Perhaps it was only coincidence that UFOs should kidnap Travis Walton barely two weeks after NBC-TV showed "The UFO Incident." The leaders of APRO, James and Coral Lorenzen, based in Tucson, quickly and strongly endorsed young Walton's abduction case, calling it "one of the most important and intriguing in the history of the UFO phenomena." (Several months earlier at the Fort Smith UFO Conference, Jim Lorenzen had announced that in the future APRO would focus its efforts on abduction cases and let competing UFO groups investigate the far less interesting "lights-in-the-night-sky" type UFO reports.)

MUFON (Mutual UFO Network), headed by Walter Andrus, cautiously straddled the fence with its appraisal: "Because of inconsistent factors, it is impossible to determine whether the case is authentic or a hoax." NICAP, now under new and even more conservative management, expressed the reservations of some of its investigators who warned that the Travis Walton case might be a hoax. William Spaulding of Phoenix, head of a small UFO group called Ground Saucer Watch (GSW), quickly became suspicious and promptly called the incident a hoax.

This cautious attitude in late 1975 by most of the leaders of the UFO movement to what seemed on the surface to be the best substantiated UFO-abduction case of all time contrasts sharply with the credulity that would be shown a decade later.

Spaulding's suspicions were heightened by a tape-recorded interview with Travis's older brother Duane, who had assumed the role of father to Travis after their mother's two divorces. Also participating in the taped interview was Mike Rogers, who headed the team of woodcutters. The interview was conducted on November 8, while Travis was still missing, by Fred Sylvanus, one of Spaulding's associates, near the site of the alleged abduction.

If Duane really believed that his young brother had been abducted by a UFO, for all he knew Travis might now be on his way back to the UFOnauts' native planet—perhaps to be dissected like a frog or to be stuffed and put into a museum. *Yet never once during the 65-minute interview with Sylvanus did either Duane Walton or Mike Rogers express the slightest concern over Travis's well-being.*

Despite the report by Rogers and other members of his crew that the UFO had zapped Travis with something like a bolt of lightning that allegedly knocked him into the air, Duane volunteered, "I don't believe he's hurt or injured in any way." When Sylvanus asked if he believed Travis would be returned, Duane replied: "Sure do. Don't feel any fear for him at all. Little regret because I haven't been able to experience the same thing."

Duane added: "He's not even missing. He knows where he's at, and I know where he's at." An understandably surprised Sylvanus then asked where Duane believed Travis was. Duane replied, "Not on this earth." After Duane began to philosophize about UFOs, Sylvanus asked if he had "read much about flying saucers." Duane replied, "As much as anybody."

Duane went on to explain: "I've been seeing them all the time. It's not new to me. It's not a surprise." And he added that he and Travis had earlier agreed that if either of them ever saw a UFO up close "we would immediately get directly under the object. . . . We discussed this time and time again! The opportunity (to go aboard a UFO) would be too great to pass up . . . and whoever happened to be left on the ground—if one of us didn't make the grade— to try to convince whoever was in the craft to come back and get the other one."

Duane said that this explained why Travis (allegedly) had run under the hovering UFO, despite warnings from his companions, resulting in his being zapped and abducted. Duane added, "He's received the benefits for it." A much more worried Sylvanus said, "You hope he has."

During the course of my own investigation I learned that Travis, Duane, and their mother, Mary Kellett, were avid UFO buffs who frequently reported seeing UFOs. More important, I learned that shortly before the UFO incident Travis had told his mother that if he were ever abducted by a UFO she need not worry because he would come back safe and sound.

After searching for several hours in darkness, Navajo County law-enforcement officers failed to locate Travis. Deputy sheriff Kenneth Coplan drove late that night to a nearby ranch house where Mrs. Kellett was staying to break the tragic news that her youngest son seemingly had been abducted by a UFO. Coplan was surprised at how calmly she took the news, as he later told me.

Travis's earlier prediction to his mother that he would return safely from a UFO-abduction came true shortly after midnight on November 12, when he called his sister from a Heber gas station public telephone. Other than being a little groggy, he seemed none the worse for his alleged experience. There was no sign of burns or injury from the lightning-like bolt that reportedly had zapped him.

On March 13, 1976, early in my own investigation into the case,

I called to talk with Pfeifer, the polygraph examiner employed by Tom Ezell & Associates, in Phoenix, who had tested and passed Travis and Duane in early February. I learned from Tom Ezell that Pfeifer no longer was employed there. Ezell told me he had been out of town when the tests were given and he offered to examine the polygraph charts and give me his appraisal of the examination and of Pfeifer's appraisal.

As we wound up our telephone conversation, Ezell casually dropped a bombshell: "Let me give you a little information that might help you. Walton was given another [polygraph] examination before George [Pfeifer] gave him one." When I asked who had given Travis this heretofore secret test, Ezell replied, "I believe Jack Mc-Carthy, who I would say is one helluva good examiner, in Phoenix." Ezell had learned of the prior test from Pfeifer, who learned of it from representatives of APRO, who had arranged the second test, which Walton had passed.

The timing of my call to McCarthy on March 15 was fortuitous because he had just received from a friend a newspaper clipping reporting that Travis Walton and his brother Duane had passed Pfeifer's lie-detector test with flying colors. While the friend did not know that McCarthy had tested Travis earlier, he knew that McCarthy was the most experienced and one of the most respected polygraph examiners in Arizona.

McCarthy and his wife also had chanced to watch Travis Walton's first public report of the incident on a Phoenix television program shortly after he had reappeared. McCarthy had heard APRO's Jim Lorenzen say that three psychiatrists who had examined Travis had "concluded that he is not party to any hoax, and that he's telling the truth." McCarthy had good reason to disagree.

When I told McCarthy that Ezell had informed me that he had earlier tested Travis, he acknowledged that he had. When I asked for his conclusions, McCarthy replied: *"Gross deception!"* I learned that shortly after Travis had reappeared, APRO's Lorenzen had called to ask if McCarthy would give young Walton a polygraph test. Lorenzen explained that the tabloid newspaper *National Enquirer* would pay for the test, which would be given secretly in a nearby Scottsdale hotel where Travis was being sequestered to avoid the news media and to protect the *National Enquirer's* exclusive rights to Walton's abduction story.

Final arrangements were worked out with APRO's Dr. James Harder. When Harder mentioned that he had subjected Travis to regressive hypnosis to try to learn more about his experiences, McCarthy asked if Travis had been given any post-hypnotic suggestions that might possibly influence the test results. The experienced examiner also asked Harder if he believed that Travis was mentally and physically able to undergo the test, and he was assured that he was.

McCarthy spent approximately two hours with Travis, briefing him on the polygraph test procedure, going over each question to be sure Travis felt able to answer with an unequivocal yes or no. When McCarthy finished around 4:00 P.M. he reported his findings to *National Enquirer* reporters and APRO's Harder: "Gross deception." Further, McCarthy reported, Travis was resorting to tricks, such as intentionally holding his breath, in an effort to "beat" the test.

While Harder telephoned Lorenzen to report the bad news, the *National Enquirer* reporters asked McCarthy to wait and adjourned to another room. When they returned they asked McCarthy to sign a hastily typed "secrecy agreement," which he did. Because the secrecy agreement was hurriedly typed, it was erroneously dated February 15, 1975 instead of November 15, and thus was not legally binding. Yet McCarthy held his tongue until I called on March 15, 1976, and said that Ezell had told me he had earlier tested Walton. McCarthy was too honest a man to deny it.

Several weeks after Travis had flunked the McCarthy lie-detector test, the *National Enquirer* ran a large feature story about his "UFO-abduction." The article headlined the fact that the six woodcutters had taken polygraph tests while Travis was still missing to determine if they might have killed him and hidden his body. Five of the six passed the test. There was no mention of McCarthy's test that Travis had flunked badly.

On March 21, less than a week after I had talked with McCarthy, I talked by telephone with APRO's Lorenzen. Without revealing what I had just learned, and after we had discussed the test given by Pfeifer, I asked Lorenzen, "Do you know if Travis has taken any other polygraph tests?" The APRO official replied, "No, never." I opted not to challenge his veracity—yet.

The next day, March 22, I called Ezell back to get his appraisal of the Pfeifer test that Travis and Duane reportedly had passed. Ezell told me that after careful examination of the polygraph charts it was his opinion that it was *impossible* to tell if Travis and Duane were responding truthfully to test questions. More important, Ezell told me, was Pfeifer's notation on the charts that he had allowed Travis to "dictate" some of the questions he would be asked. This, Ezell assured me, was a violation of one of the basic principles of polygraphy.

Thus, the results of the lie-detector test that Travis had flunked, conducted by the most experienced polygraph examiner in Arizona, were being withheld from the public by the *National Enquirer* and by APRO. But the results of the Pfeifer-administered test that Travis had passed, which Ezell now had disavowed, had been carried by the wire services and published in many newspapers. Therefore, millions of newspaper readers could readily conclude that the abduction tale was true.

My continuing investigation provided useful insights into Travis Walton and members of his family. For example, I discovered that about five years before the UFO incident, on May 5, 1971, Travis Walton and Charles Rogers, brother of the woodcutters' crew chief, had pleaded guilty to charges of burglary and forgery. They had broken into the offices of Western Molding Co., stolen company checks, forged signatures and cashed them. After agreeing to make restitution, Travis and Charles Rogers were placed on probation for two years. After living up to the conditions of the probation, under the terms of Arizona law, they were allowed to "cleanse the record" by appearing in court and pleading "not guilty" to the charge to which they had originally pleaded guilty.

From Mrs. Richard Gibson, of Heber, I learned that her father-in-law earlier had taken pity on Mrs. Kellett and her family and allowed them to spend the summer rent-free in his small ranch house a few miles from the alleged UFO abduction site. (Mrs. Kellett was living there at the time of the incident even though it was then early November.) Mrs. Gibson told me that in return for this kindness, members of the Walton family repeatedly perpetrated hoaxes on the Gibson family.

On one occasion, she told me, "they called and said, 'Somebody has killed a whole bunch of your cows. They are dead all over the meadows here.' " But when the Gibsons drove up from Heber, they found "there wasn't one dead cow. . . . It was a complete hoax." In view of Mrs. Gibson's first-hand experience with the family, I was not surprised when she said she suspected the UFO abduction was also a hoax.

If the UFO abduction story was a hoax, as I now suspected, what was the motive? Was it simply a prank concocted by young men for laughs? Crew-chief Mike Rogers unwittingly provided an important clue to a more likely motive during his taped interview of November 8 with Sylvanus when he said: "This contract we have [with the U.S. Forest Service] is seriously behind schedule. In fact, Monday [November 10] the time is up. We haven't done any work on it since Wednesday because of this thing [UFO incident], and therefore it won't be done. I hope they take that into account."

My further investigation revealed that Rogers was sorely in need of an "Act of God" or its practical equivalent, which the alleged UFO-abduction, it was hoped, could provide. In all probability, the inspiration for the hoax was provided by the NBC-TV movie about the Hill case, which Rogers admitted to me he had seen *the same night* that he wrote a letter to the U.S. Forest Service attempting to explain why he was so delinquent on his contract. In that letter, as I would later discover, Rogers had resorted to deception and falsehood.

More than a year earlier, on June 26, 1974, Rogers was one of three bidders to the Forest Service for a contract to thin out small trees in an area known as Turkey Springs. When the bids were opened, Rogers discovered that he had won the job, but his bid of $27.40 an acre for the 1,277-acre site was less than half the price quoted by one experienced competitor and 27 percent below that of another. Clearly, Rogers had bid too low. Rogers was committed to complete the job within 200 "working days," which took into account that mountain snows typically arrive by early November and extend into May. The contract later was reduced to 1,205 acres, with no reduction in time.

By early August 1975, the 200 working days had expired and Rogers had completed only about 70 percent of the job, leaving 353 acres still to do. To avoid a contract default, Rogers had requested and been granted an 84 working day extension, to November 10, 1975. During the previous year, Rogers and his crew had averaged slightly more than four acres a day. If he could maintain the same average, he could finish the Turkey Springs job by November 10— providing the first snows had not arrived. But in return for this time-extension, Rogers would be penalized $1.00 an acre on his original, already too low, price.

Under the standard Forest Service policy, 10 percent of Rogers's payments were withheld until the job was completed satisfactorily. If he failed to complete the Turkey Springs job by November 10, then this "10 percent retention" fund—which amounted to about $2,500—could be used to pay another contractor brought in to complete the job. Thus, if Rogers failed to complete Turkey Springs thinning by November 10, he had serious problems. He could request still another contract extension, which might be granted, but his payment per acre would be reduced still further. And because of the long winter, it would not be until the following summer that he could hope to complete the job and collect his $2,500 retention fund.

As of October 16, Rogers had used up roughly 80 percent of his contract extension time, *but he had completed only 37 percent of the remaining 353 acres.* There was no possible way in which Rogers could hope to complete the balance in the several weeks remaining. This was obvious to the Forest Service inspector, Tom Hentz, who visited Turkey Springs, and he so reported to Maurice Marchbanks, the Forest Service contracting officer, on October 16. Rogers already had one contract default on his Forest Service record and did not want another that could cost him his $2,500 retention fund on a job for which he had bid too little. More important, another default might disqualify him for future Forest Service jobs.

On the same night that Rogers saw the NBC-TV movie about the Hills' UFO abduction, he wrote a letter to his Forest Service contracting officer saying: "I cannot honestly say whether or not we will finish on time. However, we are working every day with as much manpower as I can hire. I will not stop work until the job is finished or until I am asked to stop. I have had considerable trouble keeping a full crew on the job. The area is very thick and the guys have poor morale because of this. . . . We will keep working and trying hard."

What Rogers failed to tell his contract monitor was that the principal reason he was so delinquent on the Turkey Springs job was that he was using his crew to work for other Forest Service contractors who had not underbid their jobs and who therefore could pay Rogers more than he could earn on his own job. Rogers inadvertently admitted this to me during one of our many long telephone conversations.

Forest Service contracts, like most contracts, have Act of God provisions, which provide relief to a contractor in the event of entirely unforeseen occurrences of grave consequence. If a UFO should abduct a member of the Rogers crew *near* Turkey Springs, it would be understandable if Rogers and other members of his crew were fearful of returning to the area. It could be hoped that the Forest Service would consider this an Act of God, would give Rogers an extension without price penalty, and would not use his $2,500 retention-fund for another contractor. And thus Rogers would avoid another black mark on his Forest Service record.

Fortunately for Rogers, a member of his crew was a UFO buff who was sufficiently familiar with the subject to be able to invent an account of what had happened to him aboard a flying saucer. But the incident would have to occur *near* Turkey Springs so that crew members later could claim to be afraid to return to their work there. If Travis were abducted by a UFO near Heber or during the drive back to Snowflake, that would not provide a reason for the crew to refuse to return to Turkey Springs. If Travis really was abducted, it is clear that the UFOnauts selected the site to meet Rogers's Act-of-God requirements for his seriously delinquent Forest Service contract.

There was another potential motivation for Rogers and his crew. As a UFO buff, Travis would certainly have read many UFO articles featured in the *National Enquirer*. Almost certainly he would have known that this tabloid was then offering an award of $100,000 for convincing evidence of even one extraterrestrial visitor and a consolation prize of $5,000 to $10,000 for the most impressive UFO case of any year. That could help compensate Rogers and his crew for his original too-low bid. Perhaps the tale could be sold to Hollywood for a movie, providing added incentive. (In June 1987, I learned that a Hollywood producer had plans to make such a movie and that the script would be written by Tracey Torme, who ardently believes in UFO-abductions.)

The *National Enquirer* did select the Walton case as the most impressive UFO incident for 1975, giving Rogers and his crew a $5,000 prize, which was announced in its July 6, 1976, edition. Its feature story announcing the award contained endorsements of the case by Hynek, Harder, and Sprinkle, but made no mention of the McCarthy lie-detector test that Travis had flunked. Sprinkle's endorsement said: "It's probably one of the most spectacular abductions that has ever been reported anywhere. . . . Thanks to the many witnesses and the polygraph examinations of those witnesses, we have pretty good reason to take the Walton case at face value." Harder was quoted as saying, "Beyond any reasonable doubt, the evidence is as valid as any that would be accepted in an American criminal court."

Harder's reference to "criminal court" was more appropriate than perhaps he realized, considering Travis Walton's problems five years before the UFO incident. Another member of Rogers's crew, Alan Dalis, would later plead guilty in Mariopa County Superior Court to three armed robberies to support his hard-drug habit and would be sentenced to serve three five-year concurrent sentences.

Shortly before the *National Enquirer*'s July 6 issue hit the stands, I decided the time had come to make public the results of my investigation. My conclusion that the incident was a hoax and the evidence to support that conclusion were offered to the Phoenix newspaper *Arizona Republican,* which carried a feature story on my findings in its July 12 edition. But the wire services, which had carried so many earlier articles on the Walton incident, ignored the new information.

However, NICAP published highlights of my findings and MUFON and Spaulding published my entire White Paper. APRO informed its members briefly and tried to explain why its leaders had gone along with the *National Enquirer*'s desire to cover up the results of the McCarthy polygraph tests.

Rogers promptly proposed new polygraph tests for all members of his crew, as well as for Duane Walton and Mrs. Kellett, which I would pay for if they passed and which APRO would fund if they failed. I readily agreed. But in subsequent negotiations over arrangements for the new test, Rogers and APRO's Lorenzen tried to trick me into having the new tests performed by a polygraph examiner with whom they had already secretly made arrangements. The polygraph examiner was a man who claimed to have run tests that showed his household plants had "feelings" and reacted negatively when he killed brine shrimp in another room.

When I discovered this effort to trick me, I refused to accept this particular examiner. Rogers flatly refused to agree to new tests unless they were conducted by the man whom they had earlier, and secretly, selected. So Rogers terminated further negotiations for new lie-detector tests.

Shortly afterward, Travis Walton and Allen Hynek were interviewed on the ABC-TV network talk-show "Good Night America." When Hynek was asked for his opinion of Walton's abduction story, he offered a qualified endorsement: "It fits a pattern, see. If this were the only case on record then I would have to say, well, I couldn't possibly believe it. But at the Center for UFO Studies now we have some two dozen similar abduction cases currently being studied. *Something is going on!*" Hynek was correct, but not in the sense he intended.

Extraordinary claims require extraordinarily convincing evidence to support them if they are to be accepted as fact. Hynek, and growing numbers of UFOlogists, were mistaking the *repetition* of extraordinary claims for *extraordinarily convincing evidence* to support those claims. In so doing, they were demonstrating the validity of Francis Bacon's sage observation: "A credulous man is a deceiver."

The trickery, subterfuge, and outright falsehoods used by Rogers in dealing with the U.S. Forest Service and in our negotiations for new polygraph tests convinced me that he would not hesitate to resort to a UFO-abduction hoax if it would serve his needs. (The sordid details are covered at considerable length in my earlier book *UFOs: The Public Deceived.*)

Four

An Incredible Abduction Tale

To drum up a large audience for its initial showing of "The UFO Incident," NBC-TV arranged for Betty Hill and Dr. Ben Simon to be interviewed on its then top-rated "Today" morning talk-show. (Barney Hill had died in 1969.) When host Jim Harz asked him for his opinion of the UFO abduction, Dr.Simon characterized it as "fantasy" and quickly added, "It did not happen." Mrs. Hill was visibly distressed and NBC officials, hoping for a high viewer rating, must have shared her discomfort.

The movie's Dr. Simon seemed less certain than the real one. In the film, Dr. Simon was shown consulting an old friend, a major-general in the Air Force, to seek his opinion on UFOs. The officer responded that the USAF had been able to explain 95 percent of the UFO reports. But referring to the unexplained 5 percent, the officer said, "I really wonder about them." On the question of abductions, the USAF officer said he had not heard of any previous reports. When the movie's Dr. Simon asked if the officer considered UFO-abductions "extremely unlikely," his friend replied, "No, I'm not saying that . . . but . . . I'd have to have an awful lot of proof."

The day after "The UFO Incident" was telecast, I wrote to Dr. Simon to ask if he had indeed consulted with a friend in the Air

Force to obtain his views on UFOs. On October 28, Dr. Simon replied: "No such incident or anything resembling it occurred. Having had two experiences with UFOs myself I felt little need to go to someone else who probably had none." But millions of people who saw the film were misled about Dr. Simon's confidence in his assessment of the abduction story, because of the implication that a USAF officer had influenced his judgment.

Millions of NBC-TV viewers surely were spellbound as they watched bald ETs with egg-shaped heads and large black slanting eyes leading the movie's Betty and Barney Hill to the brightly illuminated flying saucer and taking them inside. And many shared the terror on the face of Estelle Parsons, playing Betty Hill, as an ET inserted a four-inch long needle into her navel "to determine if she was pregnant," as Betty Hill said the ET had explained in her dream-nightmare.

The film provided millions of viewers with a script for UFO abduction and with visual images that would find a niche in their memories for their own UFO-abduction nightmares and fantasies. For those who missed the first showing, or wanted to see it again, NBC provided a repeat screening within the year, on September 9, 1976. (Not surprisingly, "The UFO Incident" has since been shown several times on late-night television.)

For those who first viewed the film in the fall of 1975, it might have seemed that *if* Betty and Barney had really been abducted by UFOnauts back in 1961, it was an extremely rare occurrence. But soon thereafter, the widespread media coverage accorded the Travis Walton "UFO abduction" could lead more suggestible persons to conclude that these abductions were still going on and perhaps even accelerating.

In the wake of the Walton incident, an Air Force sergeant named Charles Moody went public with his story, claiming his UFO abduction had occurred several months earlier, on August 13, 1975. Moody reported that the UFOnauts spoke "perfect English with an American accent," but did so without moving their lips. Moody said that a UFOnaut assured him that "within three years [that is, by 1978] his people will make themselves known to mankind."

Three women reported that they *and their car* had been abducted on January 6, 1976, while driving down a deserted road near their home in Liberty, Kentucky. According to their account, the car (with them inside) was "sucked" into a giant UFO by a laserlike beam, reminiscent of transportation used in the famous television series "Star Trek." "A split second later, we were in Houstonville, eight or nine miles away," one of the women claimed. As proof of their story, the women pointed to blistered paint on the car and what they called "burn marks" on their bodies.

With the aid of hypnosis, one of the women described the UFOnauts as looking "like humans, except they were only about four and a half feet tall and they had fingers that looked like the edges of bird's wings—*complete with feathers.*" (Emphasis added.)

The July 1976 issue of *Official UFO* magazine carried an article reporting an abduction alleged to have occurred one week after the NBC-TV movie, involving David Stephens, age 21, and an unidentified 18-year-old male friend. With the aid of regressive hypnosis, Stephens recalled that only he was abducted, while his friend remained in the car.

Stephens described the UFOnauts as being about four and a half feet tall and said they wore black flowing robes. Their heads were described as being mushroom shaped, with *white* eyes and small, flat noses but no visible mouths or ears. Stephens said their hands were each equipped with three webbed fingers and a thumb, unlike the Kentucky women's UFOnauts, whose hands had feathers. (A still different description of UFOnauts, with clawlike hands, was offered by Pascagoula's Charles Hickson. It may be only coidncidence that Pascagoula is on the Gulf of Mexico, a major source of shrimp, which have such claws.)

Still other UFOnaut descriptions would be reported later, such as those offered by two UFO-abduction claimants, named Steve Harris and Helen White, from a small town in northern California, who had undergone hypnosis by APRO's Dr. James Harder. As reported in the April 17, 1978, edition of the *San Francisco Chronicle*, Harris described one UFOnaut as looking "human, except his ears and mouth were slightly smaller and he was fluorescent looking." He said one of the UFOnauts "spoke to us in English, and he appeared to have a slight German or Danish accent." Ms. White described one UFOnaut as "a blond-headed fellow, with wavy hair and wearing a long kind of thing that looked like a rain coat." But she had trouble recalling any details about what had occurred during the two hours she allegedly had spent aboard the UFO.

Almost certainly the timing of this rash of abduction reports in the wake of the NBC-TV movie was not a coincidence. After viewing the movie, any person with a little imagination could now become an instant celebrity by claiming a UFO-abduction, as these few examples demonstrate.

The mushrooming numbers of UFO-abduction reports in the aftermath of the television movie was highlighted in an article by David Webb published in the February 1978 issue of the *MUFON UFO Journal.* Webb noted that two years earlier, in 1976, he had presented a paper at a MUFON conference in which he reported that a search of the UFO literature (covering the preceding nearly 30 years) then showed a total of only 50 abduction-type reports. But during the intervening two years (1976 to 1978), roughly 100 more had been reported, raising the total to about 150.

The surge in this type of report was reflected in the number of people who underwent regressive hypnosis with Dr. Leo Sprinkle, who had shifted his efforts from a search for psychic powers acquired via UFO sightings to using hypnosis to probe for recollections of UFO abduction. In 1967 and 1968, there were a total of three of what Sprinkle calls "hypnotic sessions with UFO abductees" and none thereafter until 1974, when there was one. There were two in 1975, but in 1976, following the NBC movie, there were three and three more in 1977. In 1978 Sprinkle worked with ten subjects— nearly as many as during the previous decade. And in 1979 the figure jumped to 18 subjects involved in 14 alleged incidents.

(In 1980, Sprinkle decided to hold the first of what has become an annual three-day conference for people who suspect they may be "UFO abductees." The conference, held at the University of Wyoming but not sponsored by it, is intended "to provide an opportunity for UFO Contactees and UFO Investigators to become acquainted and to share information about UFO experiences." Attendees are invited to present a short talk about their UFO experiences.)

In the spring of 1979, the most incredible UFO-abduction story of all time emerged in a book titled *The Andreasson Affair: The Documented Investigation of a Woman's Abduction Aboard a UFO*, published by Prentice-Hall. Its author was Raymond Fowler, a longtime UFOlogist who then was MUFON's director of investigations.

Mrs. Andreasson, a Massachusetts mother of seven, claimed her UFO abduction had occurred on January 25, 1967, only a few months after the Betty and Barney Hill case achieved international fame in *Look* magazine. But it was not until seven years later, in 1974, that she "went public" with her fantastic story by submitting it to the *National Enquirer* to try to win the $100,000 prize it offered for convincing evidence of extraterrestrial visitors.

Despite the publicity given to the Hill case in a Boston newspaper in 1964 (described by Betty Hill in the letter to her mother) and the even broader coverage in the *Look* magazine articles in 1966, Mrs. Andreasson claimed she had not heard about the incident until *after* her own abduction experience.

The *National Enquirer* panel that evaluated each year's entries, all of whose members were pro-UFO, was not sufficiently impressed with Mrs. Andreasson's tale even to recommend that she receive the annual "best case" award, typically $5,000. So, on August 20, 1975, Andreasson wrote to J. Allen Hynek, saying she was happy to learn that "someone is finally studying about UFOs. Now I can tell someone of . . . my experience . . . an encounter in 1967 with

UFO occupants." She briefly outlined her amazing story.

Hynek was not sufficiently impressed with Andreasson's story to personally investigate her case, but eventually he passed her letter on to Ted Bloecher and David Webb, who then co-chaired MUFON's "Humanoid Study Group," which specialized in reports by persons who claimed to have seen UFOnauts. Because Andreasson lived in Massachusetts, MUFON investigators there were asked to contact her.

It was early 1977 before UFOlogist Jules Vaillancourt launched an investigation using the services of Harold J. Edelstein, director of the New England Institute of Hypnosis. The first of Andreasson's 14 regressive hypnosis sessions was held on April 3, and the last on July 28, 1977. UFOlogist Raymond Fowler, author of *The Andreasson Affair*, began to attend the sessions in early June, and David Webb joined him in mid-July.

With the aid of hypnosis, Andreasson recalled seeing a pinkish light outside her home on the night of the alleged incident, after which she said four "entities" entered her house by mysteriously passing right through the closed wooden door. She described the entities as having bald, pear-shaped heads with black slanted eyes, as in many other accounts. But their leader, according to Andreasson, was somewhat different. While his left eye was black, his right eye was *white,* and he had what appeared to be insectlike "feelers" that made him resemble a bumblebee—the first such description of a UFOnaut. (Because Mrs. Andreasson has considerable artistic skill she drew the numerous sketches illustrating her alleged encounter which appear in Fowler's book.)

Another significant difference from what would in time emerge as a "traditional" UFOnaut description was Andreasson's report that the UFOnauts had only three fingers on each hand, and no feathers, webs, or claws. She said they wore dark-blue form-fitting uniforms whose left sleeves were adorned with an emblem that resembled a bird with outstretched wings—never before reported (to my knowledge). Its significance emerged, she claimed, when she was taken to their home planet.

Andreasson, a devout fundamentalist Christian, said that when the UFOnauts marched through the closed door into her house she first thought they must be angels, despite their nonangelic appearance. The leader of the UFOnauts knew her first name was Betty and told her that his was "Quazgaa." When he stretched out his hand, she asked if her uninvited visitors were hungry and they nodded. After she obligingly got some meat from the refrigerator and started to cook it, Quazgaa told her: "We cannot eat food unless it is burned." Yet when she turned up the heat and the meat began to smoke, they seemed astonished.

Andreasson said the UFOnauts then told her: "But that's not our kind of food. Our food is tried by fire, knowledge tried by fire. Do you have any food like that?" This prompted Andreasson to get a copy of the family's Bible from the living room, which she gave to Quazgaa. He in turn handed her a thin blue book and passed his hand over her Bible and "other Bibles appeared, thicker than the original" which he then gave to his fellow UFOnauts.

The tiny blue book that Quazgaa allegedly gave to Andreasson could have provided incontrovertible evidence of extraterrestrial visitations and could have won her the $100,000 *National Enquirer* prize. But somehow the little blue book was mislaid and has never been found, according to Andreasson.

During her 14 regressive-hypnosis sessions under Edelstein, Andreasson told the most bizarre and detailed story ever recounted by a claimed abductee. She said she had floated through the solid door of her house and saw an oval-shaped craft. When the UFOlogists present wondered why the flying saucer had not been seen and reported by Andreasson's neighbors, she explained that the area was enveloped in "haze." (When they later checked the weather records for January 25, 1967, they found it had been misty that night.)

When UFOnaut leader Quazgaa sensed that Andreasson was fearful about being taken aboard the flying saucer, the bottom part of the craft suddenly became transparent so she could see inside. Once inside, Andreasson claimed she was subjected to a painful physical examination, in which the UFOnauts allegedly inserted a long needle into her navel—much as Betty Hill had reported earlier. But Andreasson also reported a new, even more painful UFOnaut procedure, in which a "needle-wire" was inserted "up my nose and into my head."

(Only once before, several years earlier, had a claimed abductee reported a needle-in-the-nose experience, but by the early 1980s, following publication of Fowler's book and newspaper articles describing Andreasson's alleged experience, there would be other such accounts. Andreasson also reported that when the needle was removed there was a "little ball with little prickly things on it" on the end of the needle. This too would emerge in later abductee stories and UFOlogists would assume that the reported balls must have been implanted earlier, indicating a previous abduction experience.)

During subsequent hypnosis sessions, Andreasson described being placed in a chair molded to Earthling dimensions inside a plastic bubble, which then was filled with a liquid, and air tubes were applied to her mouth and nose—unlike any previously reported experience. Still later, Andreasson described a visit to another world, where she said she could see a distant city, and was taken into a concrete building. She described seeing large numbers of strange "beings" who had no heads, only two giant eyeballs on the end of stalks protruding from their skinny bodies. According to Andreasson, "Their eyes can move every which way, and they can climb just like monkeys." She also told of seeing a giant eaglelike bird, about 15 feet tall, similar to the symbol she described seeing on the UFOnauts coveralls.

When UFOlogist David Webb asked Andreasson if the UFOnauts had ever told her the name of the place they came from, she said they had but "I can't pronounce it." Later she recalled the name began with a "Z" and has "some S's and a P in it." But Andreasson was able to recall a "message for mankind" given to her by the UFOnauts in their native tongue—unlike their telepathic messages to her, which were in English. The message, which took Andreasson about 35 seconds to recall, was the following, as best Fowler can supply it phonetically: "Oh-tookurah bohututah mawhulah duh duwa ma her duh okaht turaht nuwrlahantutrah aw-hoe-noe marikoto tutrah etrah meekohtutrah etro indra ukreeahlah." When Andreasson was asked what the message meant, she said she didn't know and was simply repeating it.

Under hypnosis, Andreasson said she was told that she had been "chosen . . . to show the world." She said this prompted her to ask if this telepathic message was coming from God and the voice replied: "I shall show you as time goes by."

When Quazgaa finally had to depart, Andreasson said he gave her a message for mankind, but this time it was supplied telepathically in English. "He says my race won't believe me until much time has passed—*our* time. . . . They love the human race [despite the painful indignities allegedly inflicted on Andreasson and other claimed abductees]. They have come to help the human race. And, unless man will accept, he will not be saved, he will not live. . . . All things have been planned. Love is the greatest of all. . . . They have technology that man could use. . . . It is through the spirit, but man will not search out that portion."

During one of the hypnotic sessions, eager UFOlogists present asked Andreasson when they themselves might have the opportunity to see and communicate directly with one of the UFOnauts, such as Andantio (another UFOnaut whose name had emerged in one of the sessions), instead of having to communicate through Andreasson. She replied: "You would worship him if he was to come here, and that is not his way. . . . He is just a servant and a messenger."

At one point, Fowler asked if Andantio "could show us some proof that he is really communicating through you in this room—something that we would accept without hesitation as proof that he actually exists and is talking through you." Andreasson replied: "The world seeks proof. They cannot see with the spiritual eye. Only those that are worthy will see." When Fowler asked if the UFOnauts had any relationship "with what we call the second coming of Christ," Andreasson replied: "They definitely do."

In interviews with Fowler and his associates, Andreasson said that several months after her claimed 1967 abduction, while washing the dishes, something had taken control of her mind, enabling her to see into the future. As a result, she said, she "was seeing inventions so far advanced—thousands of years. . . ." If Andreasson was asked to describe some of these inventions of the future, Fowler fails to describe them for his readers.

On another occasion, she reported seeing another uninvited visitor in her house, whom she described as a "bright, illuminated being about four to five feet tall. It wasn't fat or slim. It was just right. The hands were there, the arms, the legs, and the head, but it had no features. It was just all light. It leaped down the stairs."

In 1977, at the time of the hypnosis sessions, Mrs. Andreasson's marriage of more than 20 years was breaking up, and in August the sessions ended when she moved to Florida to live with her sister. There she met, and in 1978 married, Robert Luca, who also claims to have had a UFO-abduction experience in June 1967, shortly after Betty Andreasson's. On October 21, 1977, Luca and Andreasson visited Fowler so he could meet this new abductee.

Andreasson told Fowler of a recent mysterious incident that reportedly had occurred while she had been talking by telephone to Luca. When this conversation suddenly was interrupted by a voice, Andreasson told Fowler, "I knew right away it was *them*." When Fowler asked if the voices were speaking English, she replied, "No, it was like a different language." Andreasson said the voices were "very angry" and mentioned something about "the people."

Following the telephone incident, she told her oldest daughter, Becky, and son Todd that "the beings were just on the telephone and they were really mad." Later that night, the daughter woke up screaming and, Mrs. Andreasson told Fowler, she saw a huge ball of light swoosh over her head and disappear. The next day, shortly before midnight, her two oldest sons, James (21) and Todd (17) were killed in an automobile accident. The accident itself had a prosaic explanation, according to Fowler, but Andreasson believes the angry voices she heard on the telephone were warning of the impending tragedy.

The introduction to the Andreasson book, written by Hynek, whose own book published seven years earlier had taken a cautious position on the Hill case, reveals his changing standards: "In the past, I frankly would not have touched an invitation to write the foreword for a book treating 'contactees,' abduction, mental telepathy, mystical contact and examination by 'aliens.' But across the years I have learned to broaden my view of the entire UFO phenomenon."

While Hynek admitted that Andreasson's story makes "Alice's wanderings in Wonderland pale by comparison," he wrote that "those who still hold that the entire subject of UFOs is nonsense will be sorely challenged if they have the courage to take an honest look at the present book." Hynek noted that the book "will also challenge those who [like Fowler] consider UFOs solely synonomous with physical craft that transport flesh-and-blood denizens from distant solar systems. . . . Here we have 'creatures of light' who find walls no obstacle to free passage into rooms and who find no difficulty in exerting uncanny control of the witnesses' minds."

Fowler summed up the conclusions of the five UFOlogists involved in the Andreasson case as follows: "No one doubted that a UFO experience of some kind had occurred." However, there was a difference of opinion over possible motives for reporting the incident. Fowler said that a majority of the UFO investigators believed the motive was "pure" while a minority suspected that the motivation "was financial gain—but following a real experience." Fowler himself concludes: "Just how much of the Andreasson Affair corresponds to physical reality remains a matter for continued study and speculation." And in an appendix he noted that the "Andreasson case is an ongoing investigation."

Clearly Fowler himself had some reservations about some

portions of Andreasson's story, as well he should. But he seemed to believe that at least some parts had actually occurred. In such a situation, where *independent* verification of any part of her tale is impossible, truth must be indivisible. That is, if *any* part of Andreasson's story is inventive fantasy, the entire incident must be suspect.

For me, the Andreasson case demonstrates that even a basically honest, religious person, who admits to having read UFO books and who has a vivid imagination, can easily invent a tale that credulous UFOlogists find impossible to dismiss simply as fantasy despite its bizarre details.

The Andreasson Affair and Hynek's endorsement reveal much about the changing level of credulity of experienced pro-UFO investigators during the late 1970s. Fowler's book, as well as articles in the news media describing details of Andreasson's tale, provided a rich source for other abduction stories that followed in the 1980s.

Five

Sorely Needed Experiment

If the era of UFO-abductions could be said to have begun in the fall of 1966 with the publication of the *Look* articles and John Fuller's book about the Hill case (even though the incident had occurred in 1961), as this era entered its second decade in the late 1970s a curious situation was developing.

There were claims of UFO abduction from people like Charles Hickson and Calvin Parker of Pascagoula, and Travis Walton, where the alleged victims readily recalled their experiences *without* any need for hypnosis. The abduction story that Betty Hill told under hypnosis was essentially identical to her dream-nightmares that she readily recalled without hypnosis. Even Betty Andreasson remembered the broad outlines of her experience without need for hypnosis.

Sparked in part by the work of Leo Sprinkle, there was a growing interest in what might be called "covert UFO abductions," involving people who claimed *no* conscious recollection of abduction but who said they had experienced "missing time"—ranging from a few minutes to several hours. When such persons were placed under hypnosis and interrogated by UFOlogists like Sprinkle and Harder who strongly believed in UFO-abductions, subjects sometimes described such UFO encounters.

When Travis Walton had been reported abducted, several UFO organizations scrambled to be the first to take Travis under its wing to benefit from the attendant publicity. By later in the 1970s, the prospect that there might be dozens of unsuspected covert abductees who could be discovered through hypnosis prompted growing numbers of UFOlogists to turn to this mysterious ritual. For example, after very brief training by Sprinkle, Jerome Clark, an editor with *Fate* magazine, reported he had used hypnosis to extract more details about the abduction of Sandy Larson, who claimed that she and two companions had been "dissected like frogs."

Despite Dr. Simon's sage warning, based on many years' experience, that "hypnosis is not a magic road to the truth," UFOlogists assumed that it was. No one, including Sprinkle, had conducted any scientific experiments to determine whether persons who had never had any UFO encounters could, under hypnosis, provide fanciful descriptions of UFOnauts and of the inside of flying saucers simply by drawing on information casually acquired from books, magazine articles, television, and movies.

In early 1977, two UFOlogists, Dr. Alvin H. Lawson, a member of the English Department of California State University at Long Beach, and John De Herrera, a technical writer, decided to conduct experiments to determine if a person who had had no UFO encounter could tell "realistic" tales of UFO abduction under hypnosis. Working with them was Dr. William C. McCall, a physician with extensive clinical hypnosis experience, who had used hypnotic regression to explore possible UFO abductions with 20 subjects in Southern California.

The test subjects were recruited largely through an advertisement in the student newspaper at Lawson's university. The advertisement asked for "creative, verbal types" to volunteer for an "interesting experience in hypnosis and imagination." Interviews with volunteers were used to screen out any person who had ever had a UFO sighting or who "seemed informed about UFOs," to assure that none were UFO buffs or covert abductees.

In turn, each of the eight subjects was placed in a deep-trance hypnotic state by Dr. McCall; the subject was told to imagine that he or she had seen a UFO, had been taken aboard a flying saucer, and had been given a physical examination. Then the subject was asked to describe what he or she had seen and experienced. Each such "imaginary abduction" session lasted about an hour.

Inasmuch as both Lawson and De Herrera could be characterized as "UFO believers," their expectation was that it would be necessary to prompt the "imaginary abductees" by asking them for specific details. The results of the experiment, according to Lawson, were "astonishing." As Lawson wrote in an initial report dated May 1977, "What startled us at first was the subject's *ease and eagerness of narrative invention.*"

When Dr. McCall asked the subject to "describe the interior" of the UFO, Lawson said, the "subject would talk freely with no more prompting than an occasional 'What's happening now?' " Although Lawson did not say so, this is considerably *less* prompting than usually is provided to suspected abductees by UFOlogists eager for details to satisfy their curiosity.

Later, when an "averaged comparison" was made of the imaginary abduction descriptions of the eight test subjects with those obtained under hypnosis from four persons (including Betty Hill) who claimed they had been abducted, the experimenters found "no substantive differences," according to Lawson's initial report, written in May 1977.

Lawson concluded: "This study has provided evidence showing that *imaginary [abduction] subjects under hypnosis report UFO experiences which seem identical to those of 'real' witnesses,"* i.e., "abductees." (Emphasis added.) Bear in mind that the subjects had been screened to exclude any, like Betty Andreasson, who had done extensive reading about UFOs.

Lawson first reported the results of this valuable experiment at the First International UFO Congress, held in Chicago, June 24-26, 1977, marking the thirtieth anniversary of the first reported UFO sighting by pilot Kenneth Arnold. Not surprisingly, his paper received a decidedly cold reception.

The next month, Lawson was criticized more sharply when he gave a more detailed report on the experiment at the annual MUFON conference in Scottsdale, Arizona, held July 16-17, 1977. His paper on the imaginary-abductee experiment was as welcome as a skunk at a garden party. As part of the MUFON presentation, Dr. McCall hypnotized three volunteers from the audience, whose presence there suggested prior interest in UFOs, as well as doing the same for two persons present who claimed to be abductees, with curious results. The three "imaginary" victims impressively recounted their experiences in the pattern of early test subjects, while the two claimed abductees had what Lawson called "unsatisfactory hypnosis experiences." Soon afterward, the imaginary-abductee experiment was harshly attacked by APRO's director of research, Dr. James Harder, in the September 1977 issue of the *APRO Bulletin*. Harder noted that, while Lawson acknowledged that the experiment *did not prove* that all UFO-abduction stories are imaginary, "his paper may well lead naive readers to think that there is a strong case that they all are."

Harder criticized the experiment's protocol, claiming that it differed from that "employed by experienced UFO investigators." At the time, Harder and Sprinkle were the two principal UFO investigators using hypnosis. (During my investigation of the Travis Walton case, I talked with Dr. Jean Rosenbaum, a psychiatrist from Durango, Colorado, who had come to Phoenix at APRO's request to consult on the case. While there, Rosenbaum watched Harder use regressive hypnosis on Walton. Rosenbaum later told me that he found Harder to be a "very suggestive hypnotist" who asked leading questions.)

If Harder believed the experiment was flawed, as APRO's director of research he should have proposed a new test, using a different protocol. *But he did not.* Instead, he suggested that UFOnauts might be using disinformation tactics to cover up their abductions. "Thus, it seems to me," Harder said, "that one of the needed programs of research should be directed towards understanding the confusion tactics [employed by UFOnauts] and finding ways to circumvent them." Harder believed that the reason abductees tell confused, irrational stories is that UFOnauts have brainwashed them to make their tales sound like nonsense.

"Hypnosis, or something akin to it, seems to be both the origin of the witnesses' confusion and the means of breaking through it. Here, as in other aspects of UFO research, we should be engaged in the study of smoke screens and try not to be enveloped in one," APRO's director of research wrote.

While Lawson was reporting the results of the imaginary-abductee experiment in mid-1977, Fowler and his associates were using hypnosis to probe Betty Andreasson's bizarre story and were impressed by her seemingly remarkable powers of recall. Although Fowler's book on Andreasson was written *after* Lawson's report to MUFON—for which Fowler is director of investigations—he did not even mention this important experiment in his book.

Instead, Fowler chose to quote Sprinkle: "Further emphasis should be given to the uses of hypnotic time regression procedures for investigating UFO experiences. An exciting possibility exists that these procedures can provide more information about these loss-of-time experiences, including possible cases of abduction and examination by UFO occupants."

Lawson and De Herrera recognized that the results of their experiment challenged the UFO movement's new infatuation with hypnosis. But there was still time to change course, or at least to move more cautiously. After all, UFO movement leaders and the handful of scientists who are active in the field like to boast that they use scientific methodology.

But rather than acknowledge that UFO-abductions uncovered by hypnosis *might* simply be inventive fantasy, or to seek opinions from recognized clinical hypnosis experts, the UFO movement denounced Lawson and the imaginary-abductee experiment. As in ancient times, the bearer of bad news became its first victim.

Lawson bowed slightly to this peer pressure by modifying and softening some of the conclusions of his original paper when he presented it before the American Psychological Association conference in Toronto on August 28, 1978. Although Lawson still reported the great similarities between "imaginary" and "real" UFO abductees, he now had added that "despite many similarities there are crucial differences—such as alleged physical effects and multiple witnesses—which argue that UFO abductions are separate and distinct from imaginary and hallucinatory experiences." He made similar changes in his paper before it was later published by MUFON in the proceedings of its 1977 conference.

Obviously there could not be "multiple witness" testimony in an experiment where each subject was tested individually. As for the "alleged physical effects," there are no UFO cases, to my knowledge, where the "alleged physical effects" cannot be explained in prosaic terms. Otherwise, the *National Enquirer* would long ago have handed out its $100,000 prize, which in 1976 was raised to $1,000,000 before the award finally was dropped because of the lack of suitable candidates.

During the coming decade leaders of the UFO movement would continue to denounce the imaginary-abductee experiment and ignore its important implications. As a result, hypnosis would become the UFO movement's principal "scientific tool," and "abductees" discovered through its use would become the most impressive "evidence" for the claim of extraterrestrial visitations.

Six

The Truth About Hypnosis

If any UFOlogists had sought expert opinion on the reliability of using hypnosis to try to extract accurate recollections of past events, they would certainly have been referred to Dr. Martin T. Orne, one of the world's leading authorities on such matters. Orne is past president of the International Society of Hypnosis, director of experimental psychiatry at the Institute of Pennsylvania Hospital, and a professor of psychiatry at the University of Pennsylvania in Philadelphia.

While Orne has not had any first-hand experience in the use of hypnosis for UFOlogical purposes, he has been in the forefront of those who have explored its use and warned of its shortcomings in obtaining accurate recollections in criminal court proceedings. These shortcomings were made clear in a paper authored by Orne, entitled "The Use and Misuse of Hypnosis in Court," published in the prestigious *International Journal of Clinical and Experimental Hypnosis* in its October 1979 issue. It was published at a time when UFOlogists, ignoring the results of the Lawson-McCall experiments, were embracing hypnosis to search for "covert abductees."

Early in Orne's article, he cited experiments reported as far back as 1961 that showed "it is possible for even deeply hypnotized subjects to willfully lie," and others that showed "it is possible for an individual to feign hypnosis and deceive even highly experienced hypnotists." Both have serious implications for UFOlogy's use of hypnosis. Regressive age hypnosis, which would be used extensively to probe for childhood memories of UFO abductions by Budd Hopkins as he emerged in the early 1980s as the UFO movement's chief guru on the subject, was discussed by Orne. He noted that "typically, age-regressed individuals will spontaneously elaborate a myriad of details which apparently could only be brought forth by someone actually observing the events as they transpired."

Orne continued: "It is these details which sophisticated clinicians find most compelling and occasionally cause them to testify that they know with certainty that the individual was truly regressed. . . . *Unfortunately, without objective detailed verification, the clinician's belief in the historical accuracy of the memories brought forth under hypnosis is likely to be erroneous.*" (Emphasis added.)

Orne recalled that Sigmund Freud originally believed that seduction during childhood by an adult, usually the father, was a key factor in the hysteria patients exhibited during regressive hypnosis. It was not until some years later, Orne noted, that "Freud realized the seduction scene the patients relived in treatment accurately reflected the fantasies of the patient but did not accurately portray historical events."

Orne cited experiments reported in 1970 in which persons regressed to childhood seemingly recalled the names of classmates who sat next to them. The subjects "would describe their classmates so vividly and with such conviction that we were surprised indeed to find, when we went to the trouble of checking the actual school records, that some of these individuals had not been members of the subject's class."

Orne offered a warning that should serve as a red flag to any UFOlogist using hypnosis to probe for recollections of abductions: "The hypnotic suggestion to relive a past event, particularly when accompanied by questions about specific details [which UFOlogists invariably ask], puts pressure on the subject to provide information. . . . This situation may jog the subject's memory and produce some increased recall, but it will also cause him to fill in details that are plausible but consist of memories or fantasies from other times. It is extremely difficult to know which aspects of hypnotically aided recall are historically accurate and which aspects have been confabulated," i.e., which are false.

Orne warned: *"There is no way, however, by which anyone— even a psychologist or psychiatrist with extensive training in the field of hypnosis—can for any particular piece of information determine whether it is actual memory versus a confabulation unless there is independent verification."* (Emphasis added.)

He also noted that when a subject is under hypnosis, his or her "suggestibility" is increased, "permitting the subject to accept counter-factual suggestions as real." When the same person is not under hypnosis, Orne noted, "he is unwilling to consider approximate or fragmentary memories as acceptable recall; however, in hypnosis he alters his criterion of what is acceptable and brings forth accurately recalled fragments mixed with confabulated material." This is especially germane to the use of hypnosis for UFO-abduction recollections.

Orne said that if a hypnotist allows the subject "free narrative recall," this "will produce the highest percentage of accurate information but also the lowest amount of detail. Conversely, the more an eyewitness is questioned about details, the more details will be obtained—but with a marked decrease in accuracy." The latter is the procedure typically followed by UFOlogists.

Especially pertinent to the use of hypnosis by UFOlogists is Orne's discussion of "pseudo-memories," which can be induced unwittingly during hypnosis. Orne said that "if a witness is hypnotized and has factual information casually gleaned from newspapers or inadvertent comments made during prior interrogation or in discussion with others who might have knowledge about the facts, *many of these bits of knowledge will become incorporated and form the basis of any pseudo-memories that develop.* " (Emphasis added.)

A warning that clearly invalidates the work of strong "UFO-believers" like Sprinkle, Harder, and Hopkins, who perform hypnosis, is Orne's statement that "if the hypnotist has beliefs about what actually occurred, it is exceedingly difficult for him to prevent himself from inadvertently guiding the subject's recall so that [the subject] will eventually 'remember' what he, the hypnotist, believes actually happened."

As an example, Orne described a simple experiment that he has often carried out. First he determines and verifies that the subject had gone to bed at midnight, say, on February 17, and slept without interruption until 8:00 A.M. After inducing deep hypnosis, it is suggested that the subject relive the night of February 17—getting ready for bed, turning out the light, and going to sleep at midnight. Then Orne asks the subject if he has heard two loud noises, which did not really occur.

Typically the subject then responds that he was awakened by the loud noises, and if he is told to look at the clock, he may report that the time is 4:06 A.M. When the subject is then asked what he is now doing, he typically describes going to the window to see what happened, or wondering about the noises, and then going back to sleep. If the subject is told prior to coming out of hypnosis that he will recall the events of February 17, *the pseudo-event will have become part of his conscious memory.*

If the subject later is asked about events on the night of February 17, he will describe having heard loud noises. When asked when these occurred, the now fully conscious subject typically will say: "I looked at my watch beside my bed. . . . It was exactly 4:06 A.M."

"The subject's altered memory concerning the night of February 17 will tend to persist . . . because the subject was asleep at the time and there are no competing memories," Orne said. *"The more frequently the subject reports the event, the more firmly established the pseudo-memory will tend to become. In the experimental demonstration, we are dealing with an essentially trivial memory about which the subject has no strong inherent motivations. Nonetheless, the memory is created by a leading question, which, however, on casual observation, seems innocuous."*(Emphasis added.)

Orne cited two criminal cases in which the use of hypnosis might have convicted two persons, but for other hard evidence which showed they were innocent. In these cases, he noted, "hypnosis had not resulted in accurate memories, but rather had served to produce consistent memories."

In Orne's article he noted that "psychologists and psychiatrists are not particularly adept at recognizing deception. . . . As a rule, the average hotel credit manager is considerably more adept at recognizing deception than we are. Not only does his livelihood depend upon limiting errors of judgment, but he is in a position to obtain feedback concerning those errors of judgment, whereas in most treatment contexts the therapist is neither affected by being deceived nor even likely to learn about the fact that he had been deceived at a later date."

Because of the danger that the hypnotist can, unwittingly, create pseudo-memories that later appear reliable because they are consistent, Orne urged that hypnosis intended for forensic (court) use should be carried out only by a psychiatrist or psychologist "with special training in its use." (While Sprinkle is a psychologist, Harder is a civil engineer and Hopkins is an artist by training.)

Further, according to Orne, the hypnotist should be briefed on the issue under investigation *only in writing.* Verbal communication should be avoided lest it affect the hypnotist's opinion. Orne urges that all contact between the hypnotist and subject "should be videotaped from the moment they meet until the entire interaction is completed. The casual comments which are passed before or after hypnosis are every bit as important to get on tape as the hypnotic session itself. (It is possible to give suggestions prior to the induction of hypnosis which will act as post-hypnotic suggestions)." All of these recommendations typically are violated when hypnosis is used to explore alleged UFO abductions.

Another important constraint recommended by Orne, which nearly always is violated in UFO-abduction hypnosis sessions, is that "no one other than the psychiatrist or psychologist and the individual to be hypnotized should be present in the room before and during the hypnotic session. This is important because it is all too easy for observers to inadvertently communicate to the subject what they expect, what they are startled by, or what they are disappointed by." Hopkins is always present, either as a hypnotist or an observer, during the hypnosis of his subjects, and typically there were several UFOlogists present during Betty Andreasson's sessions.

Still another precaution almost always violated in UFO hypnosis sessions is that "tape recordings of prior interrogations [of the subject] are important to document that a witness has not been implicitly or explicitly cued pertaining to certain information which might then be reported for apparently the first time by the witness under hypnosis." Such pre-hypnosis discussions, Orne warned, "may well have a profound effect" on what emerges under hypnosis.

The imaginary-abductee experiments that were conducted in 1977, two years before Orne's paper was published, demonstrated the validity of some of the issues about which Orne would warn, although he was not then aware of the imaginary-abductee experiments.

On March 24, 1980, I wrote to Sprinkle to seek his comments on Orne's article. He replied on April 7 to say he was not previously aware of the article but had now read it. He acknowledged that "Dr. Orne's recommended safeguards, his suggestions, seem most appropriate for the forensic use of hypnosis in court." However, Sprinkle questioned whether the same safeguards were appropriate when hypnosis is used to explore UFO abductions because he questioned whether there was "a crime, a victim, or a criminal."

Is it not a crime and is there not a victim if the bedroom of a 13-year-old girl is invaded and she is impregnated with the sperm of an extraterrestrial, as Hopkins claims? Is it not a crime and is there not a victim if another woman is impregnated by UFOnauts and they later return to remove her unborn child, also claimed by Hopkins in *Intruders,* his second book? (These incidents will be covered in later chapters.)

Is it not a crime and is there not a victim if people are being abducted from their homes and automobiles and subjected to painful indignities, such as removal of flesh samples for experimentation, as Hopkins claims?

Alternatively, if these frightening tales are only fantasy, there still are victims—those who have been led to believe that they experienced such terrible indignities and that the UFOnauts are likely to return again, as Hopkins claims.

Perhaps the explanation for Sprinkle's response is that, for some curious reason, the UFOnauts who allegedly abduct his subjects are a much more benign breed that doesn't engage in the sort of terrible physical indignities Hopkins reports.

Seven

"Missing-Time" Victims

Budd Hopkins is an "internationally acclaimed artist whose paintings hang in many major U.S. museums," according to the jacket of his first book on UFO-abductions, *Missing Time,* published in 1981. The jacket adds that "he has been fascinated by UFOs since 1964." By his account, he was "not particularly interested" in UFOs during his high school and college days in the late 1940s and early 1950s. But during the summer of 1964 on Cape Cod, late one afternoon, he and two companions sighted a UFO that he concluded could not possibly have been a balloon because it appeared to be moving in a different direction from that of nearby clouds.

This prompted Hopkins to read some UFO books in which he says he found "sightings like mine." (Hopkins does not inform his readers that experienced investigators, even those who are "UFO-believers," acknowledge that at least 90 percent of such sightings have prosaic explanations no matter how inexplicable they seem to the observer at the time.)

Hopkins says that, while he could accept the possibility that his UFO might have been an extraterrestrial craft, when he first read about the Hill case, he concluded it was "foolishness." However, after Hopkins bought and read Fuller's book on the incident his views changed and he "began to feel that the Hills were recalling precisely what had happened to them, and the fact that it emerged the way it did, *under hypnosis,* in two separate accounts, gave it *unusual validity.*" (Emphasis added.)

If Hopkins had read the book more carefully, particularly the chapter by Dr. Simon, he might not have made so gross an error about the "magic powers" of hypnosis. But fantasies of the mind are the source of most modern art and that is Hopkins's trade.

By the late 1960s, Hopkins had become so hooked on UFOs that he admits he would bring up the subject at dinner parties, which often would evoke reports by others of their UFO sightings. In 1975, Hopkins investigated a series of UFO sightings that had occurred near his summer home on Cape Cod, but again could find no prosaic explanation for them. His first big UFO case investigation came in late 1975, after he had returned to his New York City home, when the co-owner of a nearby liquor store told him of his UFO sighting, which had occurred many months earlier.

Seeking the aid of a more experienced UFO investigator, Hopkins soon was joined by Ted Bloecher, a UFOlogist who had been active in the field for 25 years and who then was MUFON's New York State director. Their investigation led Hopkins to conclude that a UFO had landed in North Hudson Park, directly across from Manhattan, at 3:00 A.M. on January 6, 1975, had returned briefly five nights later, then four hours later had returned again to land so UFOnauts could dig up soil samples, and then had departed. Hopkins also concluded that the mischievous UFOnauts had fired some sort of projectile that had broken a plate-glass window in a nearby high-rise apartment building, although the projectile was never found.

Hopkins next joined Bloecher in his longtime project of collecting "humanoid" reports from people who claimed to have seen strange-looking creatures. From almost the earliest days of the UFO era there had been such reports. People claimed to have seen humanoids near UFOs or walking along deserted areas with no flying saucer around; sometimes they claimed to have seen their strange faces peering in at windows. For two decades, many UFOlogists—such as NICAP's Keyhoe—dismissed such stories as fanciful. But others, such as the Lorenzens of APRO, gave them more credence.

Ted Bloecher was one of the first UFOlogists to search obscure newspaper accounts looking for such reports. A significant number of these reports of humanoids came from young children, who might claim to have seen one or two small men wearing silvery or gray suits who mysteriously disappeared when they realized they had been seen by the children. Anyone familiar with the fanciful stories often told by young children who have been raised on a diet of fairy tales should be cautious in accepting a child's humanoid-sighting report as fact. But such caution is not characteristic of most UFOlogists, and certainly not of Hopkins.

For Hopkins, one of the most impressive aspects of the Hill case was the two hours of "missing time." Had he read Fuller's book more carefully or talked to Dr. Simon, he would have known that the Hills themselves originally were not particularly surprised that they had arrived home later than originally planned, considering their diversion to rural side roads to escape the UFO that seemed to be following them. It was not until Betty told NICAP investigators about her dreams of abduction and one of them suggested that this could explain why they arrived home late that "missing time" emerged as a possible fingerprint of abduction.

So "missing time," as the title of Hopkins's first book suggests, became for him the first indication that a person might have experienced a covert UFO abduction. (Is there anyone who has not at some time looked at a clock or watch and discovered that it was much later than he or she expected, or driven some distance and arrived at a destination later than originally expected, thus experiencing "missing time"?)

Hopkins soon decided that if any of those who reported humanoid sightings in their childhood, or many years later said they recalled them, could also recall an instance of missing time, then almost certainly they had been abducted. If the person had no memories of being abducted, that was not important because probably those memories had been intentionally suppressed by the UFOnauts, in Hopkins's view. Fortuitously, the UFOnauts had not yet learned that Earthlings had discovered hypnosis—the magic key that could unlock the door to memories of UFO encounters!

But Hopkins admitted to being troubled by the fact that, in a number of cases he investigated, the subjects *were* able to recount details of their alleged UFO abduction *without* hypnosis. This implied that UFOnauts sometimes *forgot* to suppress memories of abduction in their victims. (Perhaps UFOnauts who come on abduction missions should carry a "check-list" reminder, such as those used by human pilots before take-off and landing.)

The importance of missing time, even as little as several minutes, is shown by the case featured in Hopkins's first book of a 35-year-old business-woman whom he refers to by the pseudonym of Virginia Horton. He met her after he appeared on a television program on UFO abductions broadcast in New York City in early 1979.

She told Hopkins that 29 years earlier, in 1950, when she was only six years old and living on her grandfather's farm in Canada, she had had a "weird" experience. Virginia recalled that she had been outside playing, then decided to go into the barn to gather some chicken eggs. "All of a sudden, I was in the yard and I didn't remember going from the barn into the yard toward the house." Here it was, a few minutes of "missing time," the all-important clue for Hopkins of a possible UFO abduction.

Virginia recalled that her leg itched and she reached down to scratch it. But for some inexplicable reason she pulled up her blue jeans to scratch the itch and discovered there was blood on the back of her calf. She recalled that the wound was about an inch long and half an inch deep, and today she has a scar that substantiates this part of her recollections.

The woman told Hopkins she recalled no feeling of pain 29 years earlier, but "doubly strange," she had no recollection of how she had cut her leg. But she had gone into the house and shown the wound to her mother and grandfather, who bandaged it. She admitted that there were things in the barn that could have caused the wound, but her jeans had not been cut! Even though she was only six at the time, the woman told Hopkins, she realized that there was "something very weird about the cut."

If Virginia's 29-year-old recollections were correct and even a six-year-old child recognized there was something "weird" about how she had acquired the wound, surely her mother and grandfather would have been even more puzzled at the time. But when Hopkins talked to Virginia's mother, she did not even recall the incident! (She did recall another incident, in Europe during a picnic when her daughter, then age 16, had emerged from a wooded area with blood on her blouse. After hypnosis, Hopkins concluded that this too was the result of a UFO abduction.)

One possible explanation for the discrepancy between Virginia Horton's account and her mother's is that Virginia's 29-year-old recollections of what happened as a child of six are confused and the source of her wound did not seem unusual at the time to her mother and grandfather. But Hopkins abhors a prosaic explanation as Nature abhors a vacuum.

Hopkins asked Virginia if she had ever had any dreams that might bear on UFOs, which he explains to his reader is a question he *always* asks "in cases which may have a time lapse or other clue which suggests a possible abduction." Earlier, Virginia had told Hopkins of her longtime interest in space travel and that even as a teenager she had wanted to be an astronaut.

In response to Hopkins's question about dreams that might be UFO-related, she told him that when she was about 13—seven years after her leg wound—she had dreamed "about traveling in outer space and going far, far away and meeting people that I knew like they were old friends, and I talked to them about things and they explained things to me. . . ." Hopkins, naturally, asked if she remembered how she had traveled or the type of vehicle, undoubtedly hoping she would recall a circular or saucer-shaped craft. But she had no recollections of any vehicle.

Nevertheless, Hopkins now suspected that Virginia might have been abducted at age six, and so she underwent hypnosis, administered by a psychologist, Dr. Aphrodite Clamar. Under hypnosis, Virginia relived the experience of discovering the cut on her leg, much as she had told Hopkins, except now she said, "I think my leg was cut with a scalpel." Knowing of Hopkins's strong convictions on UFO abductions, and his lengthy pre-hypnosis discussions with the woman, I suspect that he may unwittingly have planted this "pseudo-memory." For instance, while examining her scar, he may have said "this almost looks as though it was made with a surgeon's scalpel."

At one point in hypnosis when Virginia presumably was regressed to age six, she suddenly recalled something that had happened much later in her life, raising the question of whether she was really in a deep-trance state.

Under hypnosis, Virginia said that, shortly after discovering her wound, she found herself in a conversation with an elderly UFOnaut, who reminded her very much of her grandfather. Her recollections have a dreamlike quality and their contents sound very much like the space-travel dream she had had as a 13-year-old girl that she had earlier mentioned to Hopkins.

For example, at least some of her recall under hypnosis indicates she did not actually see an elderly UFOnaut. When she tried to describe the UFOnaut's hands, Virginia said that he "says he has hands," and later "I don't remember if he says how many [fingers] he has." She said that "the eyes are different than ours, I don't remember exactly how . . . and they might not have two eyes; they might have *three* or they might have two. I'm not sure about that. . . ." (Emphasis added.)

Most other claimed abductees report two eyes, which are described as being large, dark, and slanted, and they are the best-remembered detail of the UFOnaut's appearance. Virginia was not sure if they had two or three eyes and could not recall their appearance.

Yet Hopkins writes: "So many things [in Virginia's story told under hypnosis] coincided with other abduction cases; in fact, all during the hypnotic session, little bells of recall kept sounding in my mind, as detail after familiar detail surfaced."

At no time during this hypnosis session did Virginia report having seen a UFO at or near her grandfather's farm on the day she cut her leg. Nor did she recall any details of being taken aboard a flying saucer. (She would vaguely recall such details in a later session intended to explore the blood on her blouse when she was 16. But by the time of this second hypnosis session, knowing that Hopkins was convinced she was an abductee, she probably would have read one of the many books on the subject simply out of curiosity, or this could have been pseudo-memory acquired from conversations with Hopkins and his descriptions of other abductee tales.)

Hopkins concludes that the most plausible explanation for Virginia's childhood wound, and for her seven-years-later dream of pleasant conversations with an elderly UFOnaut, is that UFOnauts cut the deep one-inch-long gash in the leg of a six-year-old child and removed a large sample of flesh for some extraterrestrial experiment.

It never occurs to Hopkins to ask himself where such surgery was performed. In the barn? If inside a flying saucer, why didn't Virginia recall seeing a UFO parked in the backyard? And why didn't the kindly old UFOnaut have the decency to at least put a bandage on the child's leg? Hopkins doesn't even consider such questions. He has discovered one more UFO-abductee to add to his growing list.

Another case selected for inclusion in *Missing Time* that Hopkins investigated in early 1979 was a UFO sighting that had occurred about ten years earlier involving persons whom Hopkins identifies as Denis McMahon and Paul Federico. The incident had occurred when both were age 17. Hopkins soon discovered what he believed to be two hours of "missing time" *that the principals themselves had never noticed.* As a result, Hopkins reports in his book, "I suspected [the incident] might have been an abduction."

As McMahon recalled the incident for Hopkins, it was a Friday night and after having dinner at his home, he had driven to West Nyack, New York, to pick up his friend Federico. The two young men then had driven to a road overlooking DeForest Lake, where they had parked to discuss events of the past week and decide how to spend the rest of the evening—"where there was a dance that night and where they might find some girls."

McMahon recalled that Federico had seen a reflection on the dashboard of a bright light that increased in size and brightness. He said both got out of the car and saw "the underside of an oval UFO hovering about 35 feet above a nearby telephone pole. The object had a large beam of light radiating downwards . . . ," McMahon recalled. When they returned to the car, Hopkins was told, its engine refused to start. When it finally did, McMahon said the two of them drove to the Clarkstown police station to report the incident. Later, when Hopkins was able to make contact with Federico, he told "essentially the same story."

Because McMahon's memory was "hazy about everything" except what had happened initially, Hopkins suspected there might have been an abduction, with UFOnaut-imposed amnesia. When he later visited the Clarkstown police station, he was able to find the original report made by the young men on April 5, 1969. Not surprisingly, the story the young men told the police immediately after the incident was less dramatic than the one McMahon had told Hopkins. The UFO originally was reported to be hovering "about 150 feet over their heads." There was no mention of any difficulty in starting the car's engine. And the original report indicated that after a few minutes—seemingly not enough time for an abduction and physical examination—the UFO had taken off to the west.

But for Hopkins, the most important detail in the police log was the fact that the youths had not made the report until 10:23 P.M., suggesting there were more than two hours of missing time! Both men recalled that they had had dinner before departing for

DeForest Lake, so Hopkins estimated that the UFO incident must have occurred shortly after 7:30 P.M. Further, he estimated it should not have taken more than 30 minutes for them to drive to the Clarkstown police station, so they should have arrived by 8:00 P.M.— *if the youths had parked by DeForest Lake at 7:30 P.M. as Hopkins estimated.* But the log showed 10:23 P.M. Clearly, there was the all-important "missing time."

The police report yielded one more new fact, which I consider important but which Hopkins barely notes. McMahon had forgotten that he had *two* companions with him on the night of the UFO sighting, not just one. The "forgotten" companion was Douglas Sharkey, also age 17 at the time. Neither McMahon nor Federico can be faulted for this lapse of memory, considering the incident had happened ten years earlier. But this meant that after McMahon had finished his supper (and Hopkins does not say where he then lived), he had to drive to West Nyack to pick up Federico, and then they had to drive to pick up young Sharkey (and Hopkins does not say where he lived) before they could have driven to the parking spot.

Considering that the young men were hoping to find female companions, surely it is possible that they might have stopped at a tavern or two before they finally drove to DeForest Lake. If McMahon and Federico had forgotten after ten years that they had had another companion that night, surely they could have forgotten what seemed to them to be unimportant events that occurred prior to the UFO sighting itself. How could they know that Hopkins would attach such great importance to the *timing* of events *prior* to the UFO sighting?

Both McMahon and Federico were quite willing to appear on a television show dealing with UFO abductions being produced in early 1979 by New York's NBC affiliate station. While Hopkins was driving the two men to DeForest Lake to film their on-site account of the UFO sighting, he told them that dreams sometimes reveal details of forgotten UFO-abduction experiences. By a remarkable coincidence, Federico promptly recalled a dream in which he saw a UFO land nearby and shine a beam of light on him. Hopkins suspicions were confirmed—the young men had indeed been abducted by a UFO.

Further confirmation came a few weeks after the UFO-abduction program was telecast, when McMahon called Hopkins to report that his recollections of what had occurred ten years earlier were now "flooding back." McMahon now remembered the UFO landing and the beam of light shining on him exactly as Federico had "dreamed" it. Still better, he also said he recalled being "inside the ship and being examined by small, frightening beings."

Soon afterward, without the need for hypnosis, McMahon described his abduction experience in considerable detail for Hopkins. McMahon said his UFOnauts looked much different from sketches of UFOnauts shown on the New York television program, which were based on hypnotic recall of another of Hopkins's subjects (to be covered in the next chapter). Whereas the other subject had described UFOnauts with very narrow shoulders and skinny arms, McMahon said his UFOnaut abductors were "built powerfully . . . there were no skinny arms."

Hopkins now was eager for both McMahon and Federico to undergo regressive hypnosis by psychologist Clamar in the hope of obtaining many more details. Federico told Hopkins he would like to oblige but he lived too far from New York City and his time was severely limited. Eventually, McMahon agreed to meet with Clamar so she could explain hypnosis and give him a brief "dry run" experience, in which it was agreed that there would not be any probing of his UFO recollections. But after McMahon arrived in Clamar's office he changed his mind and declined even to try the "dry run."

This has not shaken Hopkins's confidence one iota that the two men were abducted by a UFO on the night of April 5, 1969. Thanks to Hopkins, the two have become celebrities, at least to their friends and neighbors. In return, they have provided him with two more

UFO-abductees to add to his long list. This strikes me as a fair exchange.

Eight

"Invisible Epidemic"

The centerpiece of Budd Hopkins's book *Missing Time* is a young man referred to as Steven Kilburn (a pseudonym) whose experience enabled Hopkins to make a discovery that would shake the very foundations of "abduction UFOlogy." Hopkins discovered that a person can be a UFO-abduction victim without even recalling having seen a UFO or having been inside a flying saucer!

Hopkins first met Kilburn in early 1978 when Ted Bloecher brought him to an informal meeting of persons interested in humanoid and abduction reports held at Hopkins's studio. Bloecher had met Kilburn at a Fortean conference, named for Charles Fort, who achieved fame earlier in this century for his writings about seemingly strange and inexplicable events. (Fortean conferences, at least the two that I have attended, focus heavily on UFOs with a sprinkling of presentations dealing with haunted houses, excorcism, and "Bigfoot" sightings.)

Hopkins acknowledges that Kilburn was "acquainted" with the "UFO phenomenon" but he professed to have read "little of the literature." Hopkins describes Kilburn as a "shy, intense and haunted man," who he would in time decide was a UFO-abductee, although Kilburn had not the slightest conscious recollection of having even seen a UFO.

After Kilburn had attended several such meetings on UFOs at Hopkins's studio, where he described the use of hypnosis to discover covert abductees, one night Kilburn told Hopkins: "There's probably nothing to it, but something may have happened to me when I was in college. I can't remember anything specific, but something has always bothered me about a certain stretch of road I used to pass through whenever I left my girlfriend's house." When Hopkins hopefully asked if Kilburn had seen a UFO in that area, Kilburn replied: "No, that's just it. I can't remember anything specific, but I just feel that something happened to me at one time when I was driving home."

Kilburn volunteered to undergo hypnosis to try to find out what had occurred, and Hopkins was eager to oblige. At the time, Dr. Robert Naiman, a psychiatrist whom Hopkins characterizes as having "no really strong opinions" pro or con on UFOs, had been working with Hopkins to provide regressive hypnosis for suspected abductees. But Dr. Naiman then was too busy to work with Kilburn so he suggested a psychologist whom he was training in the use of hypnosis, Dr. Girard Franklin. Hopkins characterizes Franklin as being "very skeptical" about UFOs and not especially curious.

Prior to being hypnotized on May 11, 1978, Kilburn said that, when he was in college, he would drive from his home in Baltimore to Frederick, Maryland, about 40 miles away, to visit a girlfriend. Very early one morning five years earlier (1973), while driving back to Baltimore, Kilburn said he "felt very strange," as if "something maybe had just happened to me, or was going to happen." Kilburn said he did not remember whether he "actually saw something in the sky—I believe I did—and it was there that I first felt that— something. I felt very strange, for some reason."

During subsequent trips to and from Frederick, he reported similar feelings, noting it was a very dark road that "is the kind of place that something like this [a UFO encounter] should happen." (UFO abductions almost invariably are claimed to have occurred in remote areas, usually at night, and where there are usually no substantiating witnesses.) Kilburn added: "I can't say for sure, but I believe I was a little bit confused about the time, a loss of time on that one main experience I had. It's possible, of course, that I'm mistaken." Instantly, Hopkins recognized he had another "missing time" case and therefore probably an abduction.

Judging from Hopkins's own account of what Kilburn had first told him about the incident and what he later told the hypnotist *before* undergoing hypnosis, it would seem that the discussions of UFO abductions he had heard at Hopkins's studio were influencing his recollections, which is not surprising. Kilburn recalled pulling his car over to the side of the road, getting out of the car, and seeing a light—"I think it's from the car, I'm not sure, and—I don't see me meeting anybody or doing anything, going any place."

When Kilburn was placed under hypnosis, most of the questions he was asked came from UFOlogist Ted Bloecher, who holds strong pro-UFO views. This violates one of the key principles recommended by Dr. Martin Orne to prevent creation of "pseudo-memories," which the subject later will recall as if they were real, as described in Chapter 6.

Under hypnosis, Kilburn recalled a huge "clamp" or "wrench" being placed on his shoulder, twisting it and causing him great pain. (Hopkins frequently mentions what he perceives to be similarities between abductee tales, but he did not cite any other case where the victim had told of being twisted by a giant clamp or wrench.)

Later, Kilburn recalled seeing "something behind the fence . . . all dressed in black. Can't see their faces." Kilburn said, "Somebody's coming over." When Bloecher asked, "They're coming over the fence?" Kilburn replied: "I don't know. I think they might." At one point, he said, "It's day . . . but it's night"—the characteristic inconsistency so often found in dreams, which Dr. Simon pointed out for me in the Betty and Barney Hill abduction tale.

Where earlier Kilburn had described the creatures as "all dressed in black. Can't see their faces," his description changed to "very white neck, head, face . . . no hair." He described the UFOnaut's skin as "chalkish white . . . a little tint of gray in it," and said it resembled putty. When Bloecher asked if he could see the UFOnaut's hand, Kilburn responds: "I think so. It's the same as his face, like putty or something. All the—all the fingers are perfect."

During this first session, Kilburn did not recall seeing a flying saucer, other than making a brief reference to lights that he thought came from a car. He did not recall being taken aboard a craft for a physical examination. And if an incident such as he described had really occurred in the darkness, it would have been impossible for him to have observed the details of the UFOnauts' appearance.

In Kilburn's initial session, Hopkins found details that seemed to him to resemble the story told by Travis Walton. (Hopkins does not hesitate to point out such similarities even with an abduction case that the reader may not know has been discredited.) Other details reminded Hopkins of some told by Sergeant Moody, who claimed his UFOnauts said that formal contact would come in three years—which had failed to come true. (I concede that UFOnauts have every right to change their minds.)

When Betty and Barney Hill were undergoing regressive hypnosis by the very experienced Dr. Simon, before he brought them out of the trance state he would give the post-hypnotic suggestion that they would *not* remember anything that had emerged under hypnosis. Dr. Simon later explained to me that there were two reasons for this procedure. One was to prevent Betty and Barney from discussing their recollections and adding further details to those that Barney already had absorbed by hearing Betty repeatedly describe her abduction nightmares to friends and UFO investigators. A second reason was to decrease the possibility of additional contamination of their memories by further reading of books and articles on UFOs— a potential problem noted by Dr. Orne.

Unfortunately, perhaps because Dr. Franklin was a newcomer to hypnosis and had no prior experience with UFO cases, he failed to use such a post-hypnotic suggestion to try to seal off Kilburn's real memories. For a variety of reasons, it would be nearly seven months before Kilburn underwent a second hypnosis session, on December 1, 1978. Because of Hopkins's obvious suspicion that Kilburn had been abducted by a UFO, it would be surprising if Kilburn's curiosity did not prompt him to read about the claimed experiences of others. Two paperback books on the Travis Walton abduction case had recently been published.

For Kilburn's second session, Hopkins turned to Dr. Clamar to serve as the hypnotist, perhaps in the hope that a hypnotist who was more "open-minded" about UFOs than Franklin might turn up some details about a not-yet-reported UFO and experiments performed inside a craft. Under hypnosis, Kilburn recalled that, while driving home in the early morning hours, his car suddenly made a violent right turn, "like a huge magnet just sucked it over." But later, in a dreamlike contradiction, Kilburn changed that story to say: "Oh, God! I know why I pulled over. Oh no! I see two lights in the sky when I'm driving."

Shortly he tells of looking at a fence, then that he is back in the car driving to Baltimore. Then he adds: "And I don't want to remember. I'm not supposed to remember." When Clamar asks who told him he would not remember, he can't recall. (This idea is one that Kilburn would have heard expressed at Hopkins's UFO discussion meetings.) Shortly Kilburn says: "And there's one . . . at least three . . . in front of me. And they're . . . really strange." He describes seeing fingers that resemble "white plastic tubes." Yet during Kilburn's first session, he said "all the fingers are perfect," and Hopkins had noted the similarity to the description offered by Travis Walton that "their hands were small, delicate . . . their thin round fingers looked smooth."

Later Kilburn said that one of the UFOnauts was digging a hole, that his eyes were "really shiny." "They look black," he said. "I don't see any pupils." And he described the UFOnaut's head as being like "an inverted teardrop with a big round bar on top." While the inverted teardrop shape is a familiar one in abduction accounts, the big round bar on top is unique, to my knowledge. He described the shoulders of the UFOnaut as being "really small" and "skinny." (This clashes with the description provided by McMahon that the UFOnauts had broad shoulders and were strongly built.) Throughout the incident, Kilburn said that one UFOnaut continued to dig a hole, a possible pseudo-memory created by hearing Hopkins tell of his North Hudson Park, New Jersey, case investigation and his conclusion that UFOnauts had dug up soil samples.

When it was decided that the time had come to end the session, Dr. Clamar assured Kilburn that he would easily be able to integrate his hypnotically recalled memories with his conscious memories, contrary to the procedure used by Dr. Simon. After two lengthy hypnosis sessions, there was no doubt in Hopkins's mind that Kilburn was a UFO-abduction victim. Hopkins explained that Kilburn's recollections "paralleled many other abduction reports, such as the Betty and Barney Hill case, in precise ways."

But Hopkins admitted there "was one basic and striking deviation from the [traditional] model." Hopkins said that in every abduction case he had ever heard about, the witnesses "consciously remembered at least seeing a UFO." Yet all that Kilburn could recall, vaguely, were two undistinguished lights that he first thought were from another car.

In Hopkins's eyes, the Kilburn case represented a dramatic breakthrough in UFO-abduction investigations. No longer was it necessary for a subject to recall, even under hypnosis, that he or she had seen a UFO, or been taken inside one. As Hopkins noted, Kilburn had nothing more than "a vague feeling that something he could not remember happened to him one night on a particular stretch of road." But these vague, rambling, and sometimes conflicting dreamlike recollections obtained during two hypnosis sessions served to convince Hopkins that Kilburn was a victim of a UFO abduction.

The implications for Hopkins and his search for abductees were mind-boggling, as he noted: "How could one guess how many other abduction experiences lay buried and ticking within how many other unconscious minds? If it happened once, it could happen ten thousand times and no one would necessarily ever know!"

Previously, "missing time" *by itself* did not mean a person had been abducted unless the subject also recalled seeing a UFO, either consciously or under hypnosis. But if Kilburn, who did not recall even under hypnosis that he had seen a UFO let alone being taken inside a craft, was an abduction victim, as Hopkins believed, then thousands of others who had only experienced "missing time" probably were also abduction victims. It was shortly after this amazing discovery that Hopkins made contact with Virginia Horton, who also emerged in Hopkins's mind as a confirmed abductee even though when her leg was cut neither she nor any member of her family recalled seeing a UFO in broad daylight in the backyard of her grandfather's farm.

Further confirmation of Hopkins's remarkable discovery came shortly after Kilburn's second session, when Hopkins learned of an incident that reportedly had occurred in late 1972, involving a young California woman named Judy Kendall and her two sisters. As Hopkins recounts the incident, the three young women set out for what should have been a two-hour drive back from their grand-mother's house, but they didn't arrive home until midnight—four hours late. The young women reportedly were unable to offer any explanation to their parents for their late arrival.

Later, Kendall claimed to recall having driven over the same bridge twice, *in the same direction.* Despite this, she claimed she gave no further thought to the incident until she saw a science-fiction movie in which a van was mysteriously lifted into the sky, presumably by a UFO, which reportedly gave her feelings of unease. In 1977, five years after the missing-time incident, after Judy Kendall saw a light-in-the-night-sky type of UFO and told a friend, the latter suggested she report the sighting and her earlier missing-time incident to Hynek's Center for UFO Studies.

As a result, Judy Kendall was subjected to hypnosis by Dr. William McCall, who served as the hypnotist for the "imaginary-abductee" experiment. (See Chapter 5.) Under hypnosis, Hopkins informs his readers, Kendall recalled seeing a "transparent head-shaped thing with funny looking eyes." Unlike most abductees, who report seeing only the traditional short UFOnauts with bald, egg-shaped heads, Kendall described *three* distinctly different types. One of these, she said, was a woman who seemed entirely human, which Hopkins adds "seems to be the same white-skinned, hairless type that Steven [Kilburn] described."

But for Hopkins, the Kendall case's "most striking similarity" to the Kilburn case was that none of the three women "had any conscious recollection of a UFO sighting" during the earlier drive home from their grandmother's house. Thus the Kendall case served to confirm Hopkins's momentous discovery that the absence of a UFO sighting does not rule out possible UFO abduction.

In the next-to-last chapter of *Missing Time,* Hopkins says that roughly 500 individual UFO-abduction experiences had come to light (at the time his book was published in 1981). Hopkins based this figure on his own work on 19 cases, involving 37 people, the work of APRO's Harder and Sprinkle, and the nearly 300 persons who had reported seeing "humanoids." Previously these had *not* been considered UFO-abduction cases because many did not report seeing a UFO. But now, as the result of Hopkins's mind-boggling discovery, most if not all of them probably involved abductions!

The same year that *Missing Time* was published, Hopkins was a featured speaker at MUFON's annual conference, held July 25-26, 1981, in Cambridge, Massachusetts. The title of his paper was "The Invisible Epidemic." Hopkins concluded his paper by saying: "If one wants to be truly jarred, consider this proposition: There may be as many abductions as there are UFO sighting reports." Thus Hopkins now had begun to suspect that perhaps everyone who had ever seen a UFO might unknowingly have been abducted, as well as many more who had not. If he was correct, there were many tens of thousands of "abductees" just waiting to be discovered.

In the closing pages of Hopkins's book, he wrote: "Surely

hundreds, perhaps thousands of other such abductions must still lie buried in the silence of enforced amnesia." Fortunately, the UFOnauts had not yet discovered that hypnosis could be used to penetrate the amnesia that Hopkins believed they imposed on many, but not all, of their victims.

In the "Afterword" to *Missing Time*, Dr. Clamar (with more knowledge and expertise in the use of hypnosis) admitted that after two years of joint effort with Hopkins, "I cannot say whether the experience [recounted by the subject] was 'real' or not. I do not know—nor could hypnosis claim to establish—whether the UFO experience actually 'happened.' "

But Hopkins has no such reservations. In the final chapter of *Missing Time*, Hopkins says: "We must try to make the invisible epidemic visible: We must try to take the measure of the UFO-abduction phenomenon. How many people have actually been 'used' and for what purposes?"

Hopkins noted that in his search for possible reasons behind the abductions he had discovered four potential abductees (one of whom was Virginia Horton), *all of whom were born in 1943*, "who suffered a mysterious wound" many years earlier. This prompted Hopkins to suspect that UFOnauts intentionally selected persons born in 1943 for their extraterrestrial surgical experiments. However, Hopkins did not address the all-important question of how the UFOnauts could know the birth-dates of their victims.

Hopkins indicated that he believes that the USAF and other government agencies possess "a great deal of photographic and even physical evidence attesting to the reality of extraterrestrial craft. However, there is also reason to believe that there has been *no communication* between these spacecraft and any government authorities."

In view of Hopkins's conviction that there are hundreds or thousands of abductees, nearly all of whom claim to communicate with their abductors if only by telepathy, it seems strange that UFOnauts never chanced to abduct a single responsible government or military official who could then serve as a channel for communicating with the UFOnauts.

At several points in my reading of *Missing Time* I recalled an old joke about a psychotherapist who was giving a Rorschach test, in which the subject views completely abstract images—typically an inkblot—and describes what real-life images they convey. (The imagery "seen" by the subject is believed by proponents of the Rorschach test to provide a clue to the subject's personality and inner thoughts.) In the joke, every inkblot shown to the subject evoked pornographic imagery, prompting the therapist to comment: "My goodness but you are obsessed with sex." The subject responded: "If you think those are only inkblots, doctor, you've got real problems."

Hopkins's first book provides convincing evidence, at least for me, that he has become so obsessed with UFO abductions that any even slightly unusual story he hears becomes a UFO abduction, even when it could have a very prosaic explanation. Thanks to his writing *Missing Time,* Hopkins would hear many more such tales. At the end of his book, he informs readers that if they believe they have seen a UFO at relatively close distance, they can report it to their local police department or to Hynek's Center for UFO Studies. But readers who suspect that they too might have had "the kind of experience dealt with in this book" are asked to write Hopkins, in care of his publisher, whose New York address is provided.

This invitation put Hopkins in contact with many more promising subjects and led to his second book, *Intruders,* published in early 1987. Hopkins's investigation into these new abduction cases would pinpoint, in his mind, the real purpose behind these many claimed abduction incidents—an extraterrestrial genetic experiment in which Earthlings are unknowing and unwilling participants. The evidence that Hopkins offers to support his astounding hypothesis will be examined in the next two chapters.

Nine

The "Strongest" Case

By the mid-1980s, Budd Hopkins had emerged as the UFO movement's "head guru" on UFO-abductions, overshadowing Leo Sprinkle and James Harder. At the 1985 MUFON conference, in St. Louis, Hopkins reported that he now had discovered 77 potential abductees. Of this number, nearly half (34), he said, were confirmed, while the remaining 43 were what he called "very likely abduction cases." Hopkins reported that as a result of *Missing Time* and his subsequent radio talk-show appearances, his "case load became a flood."

Of the hundreds of people who wrote to Hopkins in response to the invitation in his book, he said that "perhaps 100 deserve investigation as being possible abductees." He added that he had no accurate count of "possible abduction cases that have been phoned in to me via the scores of radio call-in programs" in which he had participated. These provided the material for his second book on the subject, *Intruders: The Incredible Visitations at Copley Woods*, published in early 1987 by Random House, one of the nation's most prestigious houses.

By the time Hopkins wrote the introduction for his new book, he reported that he now had "worked directly with over one hundred people" who appeared to have been abducted. In the introduction, Hopkins criticized scientists engaged in the search for intelligent life in the universe (using radio telescopes) for failing to "to look into the UFO phenomenon . . . a phenomenon consisting of tens of thousands of reports of apparent craft sightings, landings, photo and radar evidence, and accounts of temporary abduction and examination of human beings. Obviously the UFO phenomenon *as I have described it* may offer immediate evidence of extraterrestrial intelligence, right here and now." (Emphasis added.)

Hopkins ignored the fact that Carl Sagan, the well-known astronomer who has played a key role in the scientific search for extraterrestrial life, was one of two scientists who organized a symposium on UFOs in early 1970 under the sponsorship of the respected American Association for the Advancement of Science, which was held in Cambridge, Massachusetts. At that conference, one of the nation's most ardent and respected UFO-proponents, Dr. James E. McDonald, was a featured speaker. (The following year, McDonald committed suicide.)

Nearly a decade later, Sagan—who would welcome the distinction of being the first astronomer to find extraterrestrial life in the universe—offered the following pithy appraisal of the kind of evidence that Hopkins finds impressive: "All the really interesting UFO cases depend on believing that one or a few witnesses were not bamboozling or bamboozled" (*Broca's Brain,* Random House, 1979).

Hopkins acknowledged that for some readers his new book would "almost certainly strain your credulity." Lest readers suspect that Hopkins is too credulous, he characterized himself as a skeptic, noting that "I'm so skeptical that I find it beyond me to deny the possibility of anything." But his stated attitude is more accurately described by the word "credulous," which is defined as "willing to believe or trust too readily," according to the *Random House Dictionary of the English Language.*

For example, in his new book Hopkins reports that in June 1985 he received a letter from a young woman in her late twenties from upstate New York who had read his first book and wanted to tell him of several of her dreams. He promptly called the young woman, referred to as Andrea, and made arrangements to meet her a week later. According to Hopkins, Andrea repeatedly said to him: "Please believe me, I'm telling the truth. You've got to believe me." Andrea's worries proved needless because Hopkins concluded that "*everything* she told me seemed plausible, and firmly within the patterns of the UFO phenomenon as I had come to recognize them." (Emphasis added.)

Andrea told Hopkins that she had become pregnant at the age of 13 but that she "hadn't had anything to do with a boy at the time." She explained that she "just dreamed this man was in my room, and I was having sex with him." When Andrea mentioned that the sex partner in her dream "was real funny looking—he didn't have any hair on his head and he had real funny eyes," Hopkins immediately suspected that it was not really a dream and that a UFOnaut was involved.

To support her claim, Andrea said that when her mother later took her to a gynecologist, prior to having an abortion, the doctor found that she was "still a virgin." "I still had my hymen," she said. Hopkins asked Andrea if during her dream of having sex with a funny-looking man it had "felt like normal sex," and she answered no. (Hopkins does not consider how a 13-year-old who claimed to be a virgin would know, and whether Andrea's now 15-year-old recollections would be dependable.) When Andrea was asked if she recalled being able to touch her sex partner and she said no, the explanation for Andrea's pregnancy was obvious—to Hopkins. She had been impregnated by an extraterrestrial.

Because the jacket of Hopkins's book characterizes him as a "skeptical and meticulous investigator of UFO reports," one might expect that he would have withheld judgment until he had talked to Andrea's mother and the gynecologist who examined her 15 years before, to try to confirm her story. But he explains that Andrea was "hesitant" to have him check her story with her parents or her former physician, so he did not try.

Besides, such independent verification was not really necessary because, Hopkins explains, Andrea's story was *similar* to one he had heard from a woman who lived near Indianapolis. This woman, whom he refers to as Kathie Davis, is the focal point of *Intruders,* much as Steven Kilburn was for *Missing Time.* Kathie, a divorcee with two small children, was in her late twenties at the time she wrote to Hopkins in August 1983, in care of his publisher, after reading his first book.

For Hopkins, the Kathie Davis UFO-abduction case is "one of the most important" because of the "physical evidence" in the form of "landing trace marks on the Davis property." Kathie's letter contained photos of a roughly circular area where the grass had died in the backyard of her parents' home, where she and her two young sons lived. The area was about eight feet in diameter, and there also was a three-foot swath of dead grass running from the circular area toward the house.

Kathie did not herself claim the dead-grass area was a UFO landing site; nor, Hopkins admits, had she or her mother reported seeing anything "that could be called a craft" in their backyard. Nevertheless, Hopkins said the photos "suggested to me the possibility that a UFO landing had taken place." The dead-grass area reminded Hopkins of an incident that had occurred in late 1971 involving farmer Durel Johnson, who lived near Delphos, Kansas. Johnson had publicized a roughly circular dehydrated area in his backyard, over which his young son claimed to have seen a hovering UFO. As a result, Johnson won a $5,000 best-case-of-the-year award from the *National Enquirer* on the recommendation of its blue-ribbon panel of pro-UFOlogists.

My own on-site investigation of the Delphos case revealed sufficient falsehoods and inconsistencies in the Johnson family story to indicate that the case was a hoax and the dehydrated ring was due to natural causes, as detailed in my book *UFOs Explained,* published in 1975. Later, longtime pro-UFOlogist Dr. Jacques Vallee, in a book coauthored with J. Allen Hynek, reported that an analysis by a French laboratory of soil samples of a whitish material seemingly left behind in Johnson's backyard by a UFO showed it to be nothing more than a fungus.

Some centuries earlier, the visible aftermath of this fungus, which dehydrates the soil so nothing will grow there and which often takes on an irregular circular shape, was given the name "Fairy Ring" because some superstitious folk assumed that it was a playground for tiny fairies. Today, for many UFOlogists, such Fairy Rings have become the mark of UFO landing-sites.

In the early 1970s, soil samples from a suspected UFO landing-site in Canada were submitted to the Canadian Soil Research Institute for analysis. The results of this analysis, reported in the October 1972 issue of the *Canadian Journal of Soil Science* revealed the "UFO-landing site" to be only a Fairy Ring type fungus. The Canadian scientists reported that the "grass is often dead" because of gases generated by the fungus which produce hydrophobic substances that make the soil resist absorption of water. Naturally this causes the soil to be extremely dry and hard, like that found near Delphos and in Kathie's backyard.

The Canadian scientists noted that one possible source of the fungus infection could be urine and excretion from birds. In Kathie's original letter to Hopkins about the dead-grass area, she noted that there was a bird-feeder in the backyard and that they had "tons of birds every day" until the dead grass appeared. (During Hopkins's first visit to Kathie's home, on January 22, 1984, he learned that a hedge in the backyard also had begun to wither and die, with the most severe effects noted on portions of the hedge closest to the bird-feeder.)

Shortly after Hopkins received Kathie's first letter and the photos, he asked her to supply him with soil samples from the dead-grass area, and from outside that area for comparison, which she promptly did. He noted that soil from the dead-grass area was "hard and dry" and "lightish gray brown" (similar to the soil in Delphos), in contrast to the rich brown-black color of soil from the surrounding area. Hopkins informs his readers that "crystallographic and spectrographic analysis showed no apparent differences between the two samples." But instead of sending the samples to a laboratory experienced in soil analysis, Hopkins had the work done by Mobay Chemical Corporation's *Inorganic* Chemicals Division. (Emphasis added.) And the analysis was not performed until nearly two years after Hopkins received the samples. Hopkins often refers to the dead-grass area as "burned," when in reality the grass itself showed absolutely no evidence of intense heat.

At one point in the book, Hopkins claims that he did not at first believe that Kathie had been involved in an abduction because there was no obvious indication of any "missing time." But Hopkins finally discovered the requisite missing time after Kathie had made several trips to New York and he had made two visits to Indianapolis. Yet the fact that Hopkins invited Kathie to visit New York to submit to hypnotic regression shortly after receiving her first letter would suggest that Hopkins strongly suspected she was an abductee even if there was no obvious missing time during which she could have undergone a physical examination by the UFOnauts.

Hopkins's invitation to Kathie to visit New York, coming from a famous (and handsome) artist, UFO investigator, and author, must have been an exciting event in her then drab and not very happy life, especially because it would be her first trip to the Big Apple. Kathie is described by Hopkins as a large, broad-shouldered, big-boned woman who at the time was unemployed and recently divorced, with two small children, living with her parents and undergoing group therapy.

According to Hopkins, Kathie suffers from chronic anxiety due to a fear of the dark, as well as from insomnia. And during her less than 30 years, according to Kathie, she has suffered almost every physical ailment known to the medical world, ranging from removal of her gallbladder to the fusing of two extra vertebrae in her spine. (If Hopkins tried to verify these claims as a check on Kathie's veracity, he does not so inform his reader.)

As the time approached for Kathie's first visit to New York for regressive hypnosis to probe for hidden UFO memories, she was becoming "very disturbed about what our investigations might disclose," according to Hopkins. So he gave her the name and telephone number of a New York woman, referred to as Sue, who "was first abducted as a small child," according to Hopkins.

Hopkins explains that he uses a "buddy system" so "an abductee who has already been through such an extensive, in-depth investigation can be contacted when needed." The "confirmed abductee" is allowed to discuss with a newcomer "how one deals with the knowledge that such literally unbelievable events may have actually happened," according to Hopkins. But he adds that the buddy is "not permitted to give any information as to the *content* of his or her abduction experience."

However, there is no means of enforcing such constraints, especially if a newcomer is curious and a buddy seeks to be accommodating. Suppose you were Kathie Davis and came to New York to explore the possibility that you had been abducted by a UFO and were assigned to a "buddy" whose abduction seemingly had been confirmed. Could you resist asking questions about her experience and could your buddy resist supplying a few details, perhaps unwittingly, of her exciting tale?

Even if you (in the role of Kathie) doubted that you had been abducted by a UFO, your drab life suddenly would have taken an exciting new turn for the better because of a famous New York artist and UFO investigator who is eager to hear exotic abduction tales. If you can sustain his interest, perhaps this celebrity will visit Indianapolis, which certainly would impress your friends and neighbors. Hopkins could be motivated to visit Indianapolis if he finds your tale more exotic than others he has heard, and if members of your family and neighbors also can report some UFO experiences. But to sustain your exciting new status, you would need to extract a few details from your buddy-abductee to add credibility to your tale.

During the next several years, Kathie would telephone Hopkins frequently to describe new UFO dreams, and she would make three more visits to the Big Apple. Hopkins admits that "Kathie nearly always chooses to refer to her UFO experiences as dreams," but he explains that this is only her "efficient self-protective method" of trying to neutralize "disturbing UFO events." He characterizes this as "a useful, agreed-upon fiction." (Recalling the earlier joke about the Rorschach test, never mind if Kathie wants to call them "inkblots," Hopkins knows they are really "dirty pictures.")

Ten days before Kathie was due to leave for New York, while lying in bed, watching TV, and reading, she claimed that she "heard her name called, firmly and precisely," Hopkins reports, adding "it was somehow 'in her head' rather than aloud, but it seemed as if two voices were speaking in unison." (Recall that Betty Andreasson claimed the UFOnauts knew her name and communicated with her telepathically. Hopkins does not say whether he asked if Kathie had read the Andreasson book, which had been published several years earlier.)

Kathie reported feeling a "cold, paralyzing fear" and fled downstairs to call Sue, her "abduction buddy" in New York. Sue recommended that Kathie take a tranquilizer, which she did, but she was "too terrified" to return to bed, so she went to awaken her mother, Hopkins reports. Suddenly, as Kathie later informed Hopkins, "a small ball of light whizzed down the hall past her." Kathie's mother suggested it might only be a flash of lightning from outside, "but the ball of light had clearly been in the hall, only a few feet from Kathie," Hopkins informs his readers. "Outside there was absolutely no sign of a storm." While Hopkins states this as absolute fact, in reality his account necessarily comes from Kathie. Lightning can occur without a thunderstorm, but Kathie's report of a whizzing ball of light also is reminiscent of some of Betty Andreasson's tales.

By Hopkins's account, Kathie Davis was a troubled young woman even before she sat down in August 1983 to write to him.

But she could never have suspected what lay ahead or the potential impact of future sessions with Hopkins, who by this time was serving as the hypnotist. Because of his obsession with "UFO-abductions," there could be no more gross violation of the safeguards urged by Dr. Martin Orne to avoid unwittingly planting pseudo-memories when hypnosis is being used to try to obtain accurate recollections.

With Hopkins in the role of hypnotist, he would become convinced that Kathie, like Andrea, had been impregnated by a UFOnaut and that several months later Kathie's unborn child, whom she would subsequently meet, was removed for transplant to the womb of an extraterrestrial female. This would set the stage for Hopkins's hypothesis that an extraterrestrial breeding experiment is now under way in which hundreds, or perhaps thousands, of persons, *both women and men,* apparently are unknowing and unwilling participants.

Ten

Many Dreams—Many Abductions

When Kathie Davis made her first visit to New York in mid-October 1983, Hopkins initially focused his efforts on the night of October 3, when she said she thought she had heard her name called by two voices in unison. The morning after the incident, when Kathie called Hopkins, she said that *both* she and her mother had stiff necks and dull pains in their arms and shoulders. This had prompted Hopkins to ask Kathie to inspect her bedsheets for possible bloodstains. When she reported that there were a few tiny bloodstains near where her neck had been, Hopkins decided that "something disturbing had obviously happened to her on October 3, something only partially remembered but clearly possessing a physical dimension." Moreover, Hopkins concluded, "Her mother had very likely had the same experience."

Dr. Clamar served as the hypnotist for the first two sessions, after which Hopkins took over this role because she and Dr. Naiman were too busy. The first session focused on a *dream* that Kathie had previously told Hopkins about, which she said had occurred five years earlier (1978), involving two small gray-faced figures who moved in unison. In the dream, one of the UFOnauts, who called her by name, handed her a small black box with a shimmering red light on top, but then took it back, explaining she would later see it again and understand its use.

Hopkins naturally suspected that "Kathie's dream was a real event" and hoped that the hypnosis session in New York would reveal further details. But these hopes were not realized during the first session, and Hopkins's disappointment must certainly have been obvious to Kathie. During the next session, two days later, Kathie's tale "broadened dramatically," according to Hopkins, and began to resemble in some respects that of Betty Andreasson, as recounted in the book published several years before. (We still do not know if Kathie had read about Andreasson, but she had seen the movie about the Hill case on television and told Hopkins: "It scared me to death. . . . When I got to bed, I couldn't sleep.")

Kathie described being "floated" somewhere, with her eyes closed (which avoided any need to describe visual details), after which thin probes had been inserted up both nostrils by a small gray-skinned creature. (It is curious that the UFOnauts would insert probes up both nostrils when one had sufficed for Andreasson.) If Hopkins thought to ask Kathie if she had later found bloodstains on her clothes or bedsheets, he fails to inform his readers of her response.

If the two UFOnauts had returned on the night of October 3, this could explain why Kathie thought she heard her name being called by two voices in unison. During Kathie's third session, with Hopkins now serving as hypnotist, he was able to discover the all-important missing time needed for a UFO abduction, although he would later conclude that the abduction had not occurred at that time, but several hours later.

According to Kathie, shortly before midnight on October 3, after she returned from a short trip to an all-night food store, she discovered that she was very thirsty and decided to return to the store to buy some soft drinks. While driving there, she saw something in the night sky resembling the Goodyear blimp, with "message lights on the bottom." Even though Kathie recalled that a friend reported having seen the blimp in the area that very morning, when she said the object was "awful low" and that she had never seen the Goodyear blimp "roll like that when it turned," it became obvious to Hopkins that the object must have been a UFO.

Kathie described driving on to the store and seeing a "guy [who] was not the clerk," but she recalled nothing especially unusual under hypnosis. (Several days after this session, Kathie told Hopkins she recalled that when she encountered the "small man" she had thought: "It's crazy. Here I am about to go to New York and explore this stuff and now this happens." She added that the "small man" responded, telepathically: "That's nice that you're going to New York. It's nice you'll see your friends.")

While Kathie was under hypnosis, Hopkins asked if she noticed what time it was when she arrived back home. Kathie, who you will recall had read Hopkins's earlier book *Missing Time,* responded that she had left for the store at 11:45 P.M. but that on her return the clock indicated it was 12:40 A.M., adding that the store was only a ten-minute drive away. When Hopkins asked, "Did you get a drink? Are you thirsty?" she replied, "I never got a drink and I'm not thirsty."

This, understandably, puzzled Hopkins, since Kathie had told him that she had made a second trip to the store because she was very thirsty, yet now repudiated that motivation. Hopkins concludes that her "behavior [was] somehow being externally controlled," i.e., the UFOnauts caused Kathie to *think* she was thirsty so she would drive back to the store so one of them could briefly contact her and convey a reassuring telepathic message about her upcoming trip to New York. Because Kathie did not describe anything that occurred during the second trip that was even faintly suggestive of having been abducted, Hopkins decided that Kathie was not abducted until later, after she had retired to her bedroom.

For Hopkins this had significant implications, prompting him to observe that "this two-step abduction is, so far as I know, unique in the UFO literature." Hopkins does not speculate about why the UFOnauts did not abduct Kathie while she was en route to the store to spare them the trouble of having to visit her bedroom later.

During the next session, again with Hopkins as the hypnotist, Kathie described a throbbing in her head, but dismissed it as "probably just my sinuses." Then she told of hearing two voices in unison calling her name, going downstairs to call her "abduction-buddy" in New York, taking a tranquilizer, and watching television. Then she recalled that her head felt like it was "floating," described someone touching her near her breasts, and reported seeing "the same guy I had in my other dream" (in 1978), who smiled at her. Hopkins then asked: "Do you see anything around him? Where is he?" Kathie replied, "Just all blank, all blank, white, whatever."

Hopkins decided at this point that he had enough information to conclude that Kathie was "somehow transported out of the house and into a UFO. She is poked and probed, turned this way and that, in the typical UFO abduction 'examination.' Something like a collar is put on her neck, causing her a lingering discomfort, and leaving tiny bloodstains on her pillow. At some point she opens her eyes and sees the small gray figure once more, but this time against the blank whiteness that so often characterizes the interior of a UFO."

This Hopkins scenario ignores the fact that neither Kathie nor her mother reported any scabs or other evidence of wounds around her neck. If the dead-grass area discovered in the backyard the previous June had been caused by a UFO landing, why was there not a new dead-grass area after the alleged October 3 incident? Did the UFO carefully land in precisely the same spot to avoid causing further damage to the backyard?

All of these many inconsistencies disappear if the October 3 incident was only a dream spurred by Kathie's thoughts about her upcoming trip to New York to explore her UFO experiences under hypnosis, and if her "second trip" to the food store and her brief contact with the UFOnaut who seemingly knew of her plans were part of that dream. Kathie's recalled sensation of "floating" after taking a tranquilizer is hardly surprising. Her reported stiff neck after a restless night is understandable, and the tiny bloodstains on the bedsheets might have been there for some time.

Kathie spent six days with Hopkins and his wife in their apartment during her first trip to New York. There was time for some sightseeing, and Hopkins reports that Kathie very much enjoyed her visit to the Big Apple. After she returned home, she called Hopkins frequently to report "new and newly remembered" events of interest to him.

It would be more than a year later, during Kathie's second trip to New York, that she told Hopkins of an incident that he believes also occurred on the night of October 3, 1983, and which he characterizes as "perhaps the most important in the history of UFO research." Kathie had recalled nothing of this during her first trip, even under hypnosis and even though the alleged incident had occurred only two weeks earlier.

The first clue to this mind-boggling event came during Hopkins's initial visit to Indianapolis on January 22, 1984, to meet members of Kathie's family and her neighbors and friends. After Hopkins had commented favorably about her two young sons, Kathie said: "Budd, you know I have a daughter, too. I don't know where she is, *and I never gave birth to her,* but I know I have a daughter." (Emphasis added.) In response to Hopkins's understandable surprise, Kathie added, "I think I've even seen her." Then she said: "I'm going to see her again. I know it."

One might have expected that Hopkins, the "skeptical and meticulous investigator of UFO reports," would promptly have explored Kathie's remarkable claim to ascertain whether she was a person who liked to spin tall tales to a listener eager to hear them. But instead he chose to concentrate on other, more important matters, such as the UFO experiences of Kathie's friends, her neighbors, and members of her family.

Hopkins's visit also provided him with the opportunity to study the dead-grass area. He also examined two small scars on Kathie's leg and one on her mother's leg, which prompted him to conclude that both had been victims of UFOnaut surgical experiments during earlier abductions. (When one of Hopkins's male subjects recalled under hypnosis that he had cut his leg on barbed wire in his backyard, Hopkins rejected that prosaic explanation in favor of UFOnaut surgical experiments and commented that "barbed wire probably had nothing to do with his wound.")

A year later, during Kathie's second trip to New York, in January 1985, she reminded Hopkins: "Budd, you remember when I said that I knew I had a daughter? Well, they showed her to me. I've seen her."

Kathie described it as being "like a dream or something before I woke up in bed. But it was too real to be a dream." She said she was in a place that "was all white" and there were "a whole bunch of these guys . . . little gray guys." Then, "a little girl came into the room . . . escorted by two more of them. . . . She didn't look like them, but she didn't look like us, either. She was real pretty. She looked like an elf, or an . . . angel. . . . Her head was a little larger than normal. . . . Her skin was creamy. . . . It wasn't gray." Kathie added, "I'm pretty sure somebody told me I should be proud."

Hopkins then put Kathie under regressive hypnosis to probe for more details. When Hopkins asked, "How old is she," Kathie responded: "I can't tell. In some ways she looks like a midget grownup and in other ways she looks like a baby." When he asked if there were any female UFOnauts present, Kathie replied that the females "are the ones that have her." When he asked how the females differ from the males, Kathie responded: "Physically, not really at all. But in the way they think, the way they speak to you."

When Kathie said that one of the UFOnauts indicated that the little girl "has to stay with us," Hopkins asked if she was told that she would see the little girl again. Kathie replied, "They *promised* me." Hopkins then told her: "Take a good look at her, Kathie, and you'll be able to make a drawing of her later on. You'll remember her for your whole life." Without realizing it, Hopkins the hypnotist had given Kathie a post-hypnotic suggestion that would doom her to have more sad dreams in which she imagined she saw a daughter who had been taken from her.

In Hopkins's mind, the pieces of the extraterrestrial interbreeding puzzle were beginning to come together. During Kathie's first visit to New York, she told him that in late 1977, shortly after meeting an attractive young man, she discovered that she was pregnant. This would seem a natural consequence of the fact that Kathie acknowledged that she was "sexually active" and that her knowledge of contraception "was almost nil." She told Hopkins that plans for marriage "were moved up a few months." But then one day in March her menstrual flow returned. According to Kathie, a visit to her doctor confirmed that "she was no longer pregnant. . . . Her doctor was perplexed, but for Kathie the experience was truly shattering." She was married in April, later had two sons, and still later was divorced.

Hopkins assumes that UFOnauts were responsible for Kathie's "disappeared pregnancy," that her fetus had been transplanted to an extraterrestrial female. He does not even consider possible prosaic alternatives, such as those suggested to me by Dr. Gary P. Posner and Dr. Jerry N. Stein, the latter an obstetrician and gynecologist. For example, an early pregnancy can be lost because of a blighted ovum. Or there can be a tubal abortion in which the fertilized egg travels retrograde out of the fallopian tube and into the abdominal cavity, where it is destroyed. Or a spontaneous miscarriage may occur so early in a pregnancy that it is not recognized as such.

Equally bizarre, Hopkins also concludes that Kathie had not been impregnated by her boyfriend as she believed, but rather by UFOnauts using extraterrestrial sperm. Under hypnosis Kathie recalled that in late 1977, exact date unknown, she and two teenage girlfriends had gone for a drive in the country and had seen a UFO that she said at first looked like an airplane with flashing strobe anti-collision lights. In a rambling, almost incoherent account, she described how she and one of her friends, Dorothy, got out of the car to look at the UFO, which she at one point described as resembling a *black cloud*. Then she described being prone, her legs floating, and feeling "hot from the waist down" and something "like a finger" where her "uterus is."

Hopkins was frustrated because Kathie could not describe any visual images, claiming her eyes were shut, so he used what he calls a "curtain trick" to prompt her. As a result, Kathie then described seeing a room, and after more prompting by Hopkins, she said she saw a balcony. Then she reported seeing UFOnauts, but when Hopkins asked what they looked like, Kathie responded: "I don't see 'em. I hear 'em." When he asked what was happening, Kathie said her legs were up on a step, but she added: "Feels good. They just told me to rest."

The explanation is clear to Hopkins: "She had been penetrated by a probe of some sort that had gone deep inside her," to impregnate her with extraterrestrial sperm.

Hopkins did not probe for details of the removal of Kathie's fetus until her third visit to New York, in October 1985, when she suggested to him that it might have occurred one night in early 1978 while she was visiting at the home of a married sister. Under hypnosis administered by Hopkins, she described lying on the sofa late one evening watching television. Then she described feeling "like a flower opened up . . . all my female stuff." When Hopkins asked if she felt "anything in you," she replied: "Something very large." When Hopkins asked if the something was hard or pliable, Kathie responded: "Just hard."

Hopkins asked if the encounter felt like a medical pelvic examination, and Kathie replied, "Sort of," but added that "it doesn't hurt." When he asked how she would describe the procedure, she replied, "Slow, gentle like." Then she complained that her back was hurting and she groaned, then that her stomach was being squashed. When she said she wanted to scream and Hopkins asked why, Kathie cried out: "It's not fair! It's mine! It's mine! I hate you. I hate you! . . . It's not fair."

Hopkins said he guessed what had happened and soon after he brought Kathie out of hypnosis she confirmed his suspicions: "They had taken her baby." He said he tried to comfort her, saying that "what they had done was cruel," but Kathie continued to sob, with tears flooding down her face. When she had calmed down a bit, Hopkins asked if she had told the UFOnauts that their actions were cruel and that they had no right to take her baby. She replied, "I screamed it at them," adding "and the fucker looked surprised."

Hopkins says that he consulted with Dr. John Burger, whom he identifies as "director of gynecology and obstetrics at New Jersey's Perth Amboy Hospital." (Dr. Eumena Divino holds that position and Dr. Burger is instead the director of outpatient gynecology and obstetrics at the hospital, whose name was changed in 1984 to the Raritan Bay Medical Center.) If Dr. Burger was consulted on the possibility of removing a several-month-old fetus without fatal consequences in the unsterile environment of Kathie's sister's home and safely transporting it to an extraterrestrial mother, Hopkins fails to so inform his readers.

Hopkins was pleased that he now had all the circumstantial evidence he needed to confirm his fantasy of an extraterrestrial interbreeding experiment—but I fear that Kathie may bear mental scars for as long as she lives.

In the spring of 1986, Kathie called Hopkins to report another remarkable *dream,* which led to her fourth visit to New York in May. Hopkins notes that he was not really surprised at Kathie's latest dream because UFOnauts "have time and time again involved themselves in her life and in the lives of other members of her family."

Kathie told Hopkins that in her latest dream she had been shown a tiny baby as well as the little girl she earlier had dreamed of seeing. According to Hopkins, in the dream Kathie was told that these two children "presumably her own—were but two of *nine.* The implication was that since 1978, *nine* of her ova had been taken, successfully fertilized and brought to term." Despite the seeming cruelty and insensitivity of the UFOnauts in performing their experiments,

Hopkins notes that "in a strangely personal, human note, she was told that she would be allowed to *name* the children!"

Hopkins recalls that in November 1983, following Kathie's first visit to New York, she had called to tell him of her three-year-old son Tommy's massive nosebleed, which his doctor attributed to a self-induced puncture by a pencil or similar object, but which Hopkins suspected was a UFOnaut nostril probe. At that time, Kathie told him of her own recent dream of "laying on a table" and seeing "the same guy I've seen before, with the big eyes." In the dream, she told Hopkins, the "guy" had his hand on her abdomen and asked her how she was feeling, to which she replied that she was tired and "kind of crampy."

When Hopkins consulted with Dr. Burger, he described the medical procedure for removing ova for "test-tube babies." The ovum is fertilized outside the uterus and then implanted in a host mother. To remove an ovum, a needle is inserted in a woman's abdomen to introduce a gas, such as carbon dioxide. Then another instrument is inserted into the navel to remove the ovum. Dr. Burger told Hopkins: "It sounds to me like your friends in the UFOs may be removing ova from women who aren't even aware of it, and they're using a method very much like ours." If Hopkins thought to ask Kathie whether she later had noticed a scab on her navel or blood stains on the bedsheets, he fails to inform his readers.

All the pieces of the puzzle now fit neatly into place, in Hopkins's mind, prompting him to write that the "implications of this kind of genetic experiment are obviously profound." He speculates that the breeding of Earthling-ET hybrids may be intended to acclimate "their species to our planet and our atmosphere." But so far as Hopkins notes in his book, none of his subjects reported that their UFOnauts were wearing spacesuits with special life-support systems like those our astronauts used when they landed on the moon. This indicates that, if UFOnauts exist, then they must come from a planet much like our own. And they must be a very similar species if ova and unborn fetuses from Earthlings can be readily transplanted to their females.

Another possibility, he suggests, is that the UFOnauts "simply want to acquire some of our genetic characteristics . . . to enrich their stock." Hopkins fails to consider that the UFOnauts' choice of Kathie Davis to play "queen-bee" would be a poor one if Hopkins believes what Kathie told him about her many, many physical disabilities.

Kathie said she had had a problem with her weight since childhood, seemingly the result of a hormonal imbalance, and by the age of ten was suffering from high blood pressure. At age fourteen she had an operation for gallstones and had her gallbladder removed. She said she suffered from hepatitis and almost died of pneumonia. Just prior to the birth of her first son, she suffered kidney failure; and she reportedly has two extra vertebrae in her spine that mysteriously fused. When her appendix was removed, the surgeon discovered cysts on her ovaries. Shortly before she first wrote to Hopkins, she was hospitalized for a severe asthma attack and one of her lungs collapsed. Later she showed an arrhythmic heartbeat.

If Hopkins's theory of an extraterrestrial genetic experiment is correct, then the choice of Kathie as a subject suggests that the objective might be to *degrade* the health of extraterrestrials, perhaps to *reduce* their lifespan to solve an overpopulation problem. But if that were their objective, it would be so much easier to abduct Kathie and take her back to their native planet than to have to make the long journey to Earth every time they wanted another of her ova.

Hopkins is convinced that the extraterrestrial genetic experiment is multifaceted, because some of his male subjects describe having been "raped" by female extraterrestrials. One such "victim" described his sex-partner as having long black hair, while another subject said his extraterrestrial sex-mate had a large *bald* head but was quite voluptuous.

Hopkins does not even consider the possibility that these stories might be sexual dream fantasies, even when they contain obvious contradictions. For example, one male subject reported that after his encounter, his sex partner left the room while "two guys . . . took little spoons and scraped the leftover semen off my penis" and put it in a bottle. But later the subject told Hopkins: "I'm sterile. They didn't even get any sperm. I had a vasectomy a couple of years before this." This prompts Hopkins to recall that after a previous hypnosis session this subject had said that the UFOnauts seemed angry at him. "Now I understood why," Hopkins writes.

If these tales are not simply fantasy, it seems to me that the UFOnauts selected to carry out this important extraterrestrial genetic experiment are a bunch of incompetent dum-dums! Imagine them selecting Kathie Davis as their queen-bee, instead of someone like Jane Fonda or Dolly Parton! But Hopkins conveniently ignores such obvious flaws in his theory.

Hopkins tells his readers that there is a long-term impact, especially for those who believe they have been abducted more than once. This impact was described by a young woman from Minnesota, who Hopkins claims has been abducted twice, once as a child: "For most of us, it began as memories. Though some of us recalled parts or all of our experiences, it was more common for us to have to seek them out where they were—buried in a form of amnesia. Often we did this through hypnosis, which was, for many of us, a new experience. . . . Almost without exception we felt terrified as we relived these traumatic events. . . . But there was also disbelief. *This can't be real.* . . . We often felt crazy."

The young woman revealed her ambivalent feelings in the following words: "The people we talked to believed us and doubted us. . . . Many were rigid in their denial of even the slightest possibility of abductions. . . . We felt caught in the prison of a vicious circle that seemed to be imposed on us as abductees by a skeptical society. . . . What finally dawned on us was that others had no proof that the abductions *weren't* real. If the thought of abduction was so threatening to them, that was their problem, not ours."

But she admitted that "after the abductions surfaced, we experienced insomnia, headaches, exhaustion, changes in appetite and a renewed sense of fear and powerlessness. *If an abduction happened once it could happen again, at any time, without warning, and there was nothing we could do to prevent it."* (Emphasis added.)

During Kathie's fourth visit to New York, in May 1986, she and 15 other "abductees" met in Hopkins's studio to discuss the impact of their experiences on their personal lives. After summarizing her "disappeared pregnancy," the removal of her unborn child by UFOnauts, and her subsequent meeting with her "hybrid daughter," Kathie said: "They told me that I would see her again. That's why I don't want them *not* to come back . . . on the slim chance that this is not . . . just a dream. That's something I don't want to miss out on." Hopkins adds: "Kathie's sadness and bitterness filled her, and for a while we all sat in silence." I too was filled with sadness for Kathie.

Hopkins concludes his book by saying "None of us knows what the UFO phenomenon really is or what its ultimate purposes may be, but in the absence of answers, we must at least act upon our feelings. In place of the simple-minded ridicule and dismissal so often encountered, we must offer understanding and heartfelt emotional support to these fellow human beings who have endured such profoundly unsettling, unfathomable, truly alien experiences. They are, in every sense of the word, victims."

Indeed they are. But needlessly so, in my opinion. When Betty and Barney Hill finished their treatment under Dr. Simon, the experienced psychiatrist assured them that the UFO-abduction tale was simply dream-fantasy. He thereby freed them from the cloud of perpetual fear that they might again encounter such a potentially terrifying experience. And while Betty Hill subsequently claimed that she often saw UFOs in the night sky, neither she nor Barney lived in fear of repeated abductions.

This contrasts sharply with Hopkins's subjects. For example, after one male subject, a New York City policeman, recounted under hypnosis his "rape" by a gruesome-looking extraterrestrial female, he said to Hopkins: "It was a dream, wasn't it, Budd? It had to be a dream. . . . This can't be real, can it?" Hopkins says he reassured the subject that it was only a dream, but adds that "as I spoke there were tears in his eyes, and in mine, *because we both knew the truth.*" (Emphasis added.) Hopkins admits that "every single abductee I've ever worked with is sure that it may happen again."

How tragic for those who have sought counsel from a person with no training in psychotherapy who admits that he has shifted his emphasis to "therapeutic considerations—helping the abductee deal with fear and uncertainty." In my opinion, that fear and uncertainty is the completely unnecessary product of Hopkins's own UFO fantasies, which he unwittingly implants in his subjects' minds. When subjects are under hypnosis and thus in an extremely suggestible state of mind, pseudo-memories unwittingly implanted can last a lifetime.

Eleven

Psychological Profile

In the fall of 1981, following publication of Hopkins's first book, arrangements were made to have nine "abductees" undergo extensive personality tests by Dr. Elizabeth Slater, a psychologist experienced in such testing. The Fund for UFO Research (FUFOR), headed by Dr. Bruce S. Maccabee, a Navy physicist, agreed to provide funds for the tests. Quite properly, Dr. Slater was *not* told in advance that Hopkins believed all of the test subjects were victims of UFO-abductions. Instead, she was simply told that the sponsor was interested in trying to assess the similarities and differences between members of the group, as well as their psychological strengths and weaknesses.

In requesting financial support from FUFOR to conduct the tests, Hopkins, Bloecher, and Dr. Clamar suggested that the tests could show whether the subjects had some type of mental disorder that could explain their "bizarre stories," according to a report on the tests published by FUFOR in 1985. A second objective was to determine if "certain psychological characteristics or physical attributes might predispose one to such an experience." That is, whether UFOnauts are "looking for particular types of people to abduct." Finally, they could ascertain whether there were certain types of "psychic scars" in people who thought they had been abducted.

As each of the subjects was tested, Slater submitted a report to Clamar. When the testing of all nine was completed, she submitted a 15-page report, in June 1983, entitled "Conclusions on Nine Psychologicals." (Because Kathie Davis did not write Hopkins until August 1983, she was not one of those tested.) Only after Slater had submitted her report was she told of the motivations behind the test, which was a scientifically appropriate protocol.

When FUFOR published a 49-page report on the tests, it included an introduction by Maccabee and two commentaries by Dr. Ronald Westrum, a professor of sociology at Eastern Michigan University. A profile of the nine test subjects showed that their ages ranged from about 25 to 40. Five of the subjects were male, four of them divorced and the fifth unmarried. Three of the four females were unmarried. All of the subjects had college educations and three had post-graduate education. Hopkins was convinced that all of the subjects had been abducted at least once; he suspected that most had experienced multiple encounters and that one man had been abducted at least four times, beginning in 1957 at the age of two.

In Dr. Slater's original 15-page report, she noted the following similarities among the nine subjects tested:

1. They were above average in intelligence and were a "very distinctive, unusual and interesting" group who, except for one subject, "did *not* represent an ordinary cross-section of the population." (Emphasis added.)

2. "At their best, they are highly inventive, creative and original. At their worst, they are beset by intense emotional upheaval." She noted that several individuals in the group could be characterized as "eccentric or odd."

3. Under stressful conditions at least six of the nine subjects showed a "potential for more or less transient psychotic experiences involving a loss of reality testing along with confused and disordered thinking that can be bizarre."

4. All nine exhibited "a modicum of . . . narcissistic disturbance.

It is manifest along at least three dimensions: identity disturbance, lowered self-esteem, relative egocentricity and/or lack of emotional maturity." She noted that identity disturbance was particularly apparent in terms of "sexual identity confusion."

5. As a group, the subjects "lack solidity and coherence in their experience of selfhood." In this respect, Slater noted that "it is striking" that their "difficulties are so like those one sees in the consulting room," i.e., in patients who have sought help from psychotherapists.

6. The group contained a wide spectrum of personality types. "Some were flamboyantly exhibitionistic and dramatic with an exaggerated display of emotions. . . . Others were quite shy, sensitive and reticent."

7. All but one of the subjects showed a "tendency toward mildly paranoid thinking." Dr. Slater emphasized this was not "blatant paranoid symptomatology but rather oversensitivity, defensiveness and fear of criticism, and susceptibility to feeling pressured."

To obtain an independent appraisal of Slater's findings, I sent a copy of the FUFOR report to Dr. Marc Nissenson and Norma Nissenson, in Highland Park, Illinois, both psychotherapists licensed in the state of Illinois. Their appraisal is summarized as follows: "Individuals displaying the type of psychopathological syndrome described by the testing psychologist may under intrapsychic stress believe they have experienced exotic events such as hallucinated UFO abduction."

I also sent a copy of the FUFOR report to Dr. Terence Hines, assistant professor of psychology at Pace University, Pleasantville, New York, for his comments. He noted that Slater found the subjects to have a "considerable flexibility of thought and sensitivity to . . . fantasy." This prompted Hines to comment that such persons would be inclined to have dreams or fantasies that they "may or may not have at first believed to be real. However, after their interactions with Budd Hopkins and his leading questions, hypnosis and reinforcement for further stories and details, they came to believe, in most cases, that what they had experienced was real."

If Hopkins and Bloecher expected that the psychological tests would show that the nine "abductees" were a representative cross-section of the population, Slater's report must have been a shattering disappointment. In an effort to reconcile their UFO-abduction convictions with the test results, they came up with a possible explanation: Perhaps the unusual personality characteristics were the *result* of having been abducted by a UFO.

So after Slater was told of the underlying objectives of the tests she had conducted she was asked to read Hopkins's book *Missing Time* and then to write an addendum that considered whether a UFO-abduction could possibly have caused the personality characteristics observed.

For Slater this would necessarily be pure speculation because there are no confirmed UFO-abduction victims and certainly none who had been tested before and after such an encounter to assess its psychological impact. Thus Slater's speculations necessarily would be strongly influenced by what she read in *Missing Time* and what she was told by Hopkins and Bloecher. The result of Slater's speculative response was an eight-page addendum, completed October 30, 1983, also contained in the FUFOR report. In it, Slater concluded that the subjects' reported UFO experiences could not be explained on the basis of severe mental disorders. She reported no evidence that the subjects were pathological liars or paranoid schizophrenics. With reference to this, the Nissensons state that "Dr. Slater seems to have chosen inappropriate categories of mental disturbance and also appears to have overlooked significant pathology she herself had reported in her [original] findings." The Nissensons add: "One does not have to be certifiably insane to believe in UFO experiences. There are other emotional disturbances, states and conditions that make one vulnerable to the development of such mistaken beliefs and/or misperceptions."

Slater cited two other possibilities, "fugue states" and "multiple personalities," both based on a psychological mechanism known as "dissociation," but reported finding no evidence of it in the tests.

Plate 1

Plate 2

Plate 1: Betty Hill, who attracted international attention to claims of "UFO-abduction" in 1966 after dreaming that she and her husband Barney were abducted by spacemen following a UFO sighting. (See Chapter 1.)

Plate 2: Charles Hickson, of Pascagoula, Miss., was the next "abductee" to become an instant celebrity in fall of 1973 when he claimed that he and a young companion were taken aboard a flying saucer for a superficial physical examination. (See Chapter 2.)

Plate 3

Plate 3: In the fall of 1975, millions of NBC-TV viewers saw a dramatic two-hour special that presented Betty Hill's abduction dreams as reality and misrepresented the views of her psychiatrist, Dr. Ben Simon. The film was shown again the following year and has been repeated several times since then. (See Chapter 4.)

Plate 4

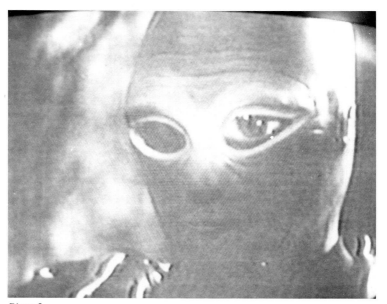

Plate 5

Plates 4-5: Millions of persons who saw the NBC-TV show learned that UFOnauts are shorter than Earthlings and have large, bald heads and large slanting eyes. This stereotype would emerge in many claims of UFO-abduction that were made shortly after the TV program was aired.

Plate 6

Plate 7

Plate 8

Plate 9

Plate 10

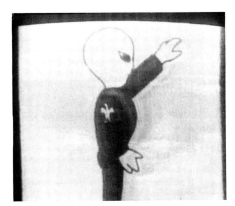

Plate 11

Plates 6-11: Sketches of UFOnauts made by "abductees" or by artists under their direction show the influence of the stereotype used in the NBC-TV show and in science fiction books and movies. But tales told by many claimants differ sharply.

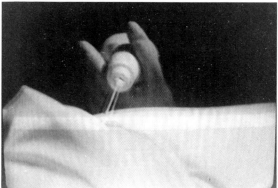

Plate 12

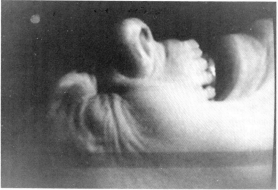

Plate 13

Plates 12-13: In Betty Hill's UFO-abduction nightmare, she dreamed that a long needle was inserted into her abdomen to determine whether she was pregnant. This detail was vividly shown in the NBC-TV film—as was the pain on the face of actress Estelle Parsons, who played Betty Hill. Not surprisingly, some abduction claimants would later report similar tests.

Plate 14

Plate 14: Less than three weeks after the NBC-TV show first aired, Travis Walton—a young Arizona woodcutter—claimed to have been "zapped" by a UFO, abducted, and given a superficial physical examination. Five days later he reappeared with no scars or other physical evidence to substantiate his tale. Several weeks earlier he had told his mother that if he ever was abducted by a UFO she need not worry because he would return safely. (See Chapter 3.)

Plate 15

Plate 15: "Kathie Davis" is the centerpiece of Budd Hopkins's book *Intruders,* in which he reports on his 12 years of investigations into claims of UFO-abduction. Hopkins believes, based on her dreams, that Davis was the unwilling participant in an extraterrestrial genetic experiment. She does not concur with his appraisal.

Plate 16

Plate 16: Hopkins believes the "Kathie Davis" incident to be one of the most important and convincing UFO-abduction cases because of an area of dead grass in Davis's back yard where he is convinced that a UFO landed, despite the fact that nobody saw anything resembling a craft there. The dead-grass area appears to be nothing more than a fungus growth commonly referred to as a "fairy ring." (See Chapters 9-10.)

Plate 17

Plate 17: Although Hopkins uses pseudonyms for all of the "abductees" referred to in his book, at least a few eagerly appear on national TV programs using their real names. Shown here are Connie Morgan (left) and Dorothy Wallis, who appeared with Hopkins on the "Oprah Winfrey Show." Wallis claims that she was abducted twice in her youth and that the UFOnauts extracted ova on one occasion. (See Chapter 12.)

Plate 18   Plate 19

Plates 18-19: Two more of Hopkins's subjects who have appeared on national TV under their true names are Kris Florence and Mike Shea. Florence expressed doubt over Hopkins's conclusion that her unborn child had been removed by UFOnauts and Shea said he is not convinced that he has been abducted numerous times, as Hopkins believes.

Plate 20

Plate 21

Plates 20-21: Hopkins, who has emerged as the world's leading "abductionist" as a result of his 12 years of work in the field of "UFO-abductions," is shown (left) during one of his frequent TV talk-show appearances and (right) at the 1987 conference of the Mutual UFO Network (MUFON). (See Chapter 15.)

Plate 22

Plate 23

Plate 22 (L): Whitley Strieber, originally one of Hopkins's subjects, was paid one million dollars for his book *Communion,* in which he describes his "UFO-abduction" experiences. He plans to form a group to investigate such incidents. This photo was taken at the 1987 MUFON conference. (See Chapters 13-14.)

Plate 23 (R): David Jacobs, who has served as the historian of the UFO movement and earlier cautioned about accepting claims of UFO-abduction, more recently has become an active "abductionist" and understudy to Hopkins. (See Chapter 15.)

Plate 24

Plate 25

Plate 26

Plates 24-26: The 1987 MUFON conference featured a "UFO-abduction" session with eight panelists. At the extreme left in the top photo is Whitley Strieber and at the far right is Charles Hickson. Plate 25 shows (l.-r.): Kris Florence, "Susan Taylor," and Peter Robbins. (See Chapter 17.) Plate 26: Mike Shea, "Kathie Davis," and Rosemary Osnato.

However, she cautioned that dissociation "is very subtle and difficult to detect . . . and careful interviewing is needed to firmly rule out its presence."

Slater said that while the tests she had conducted "can do nothing to prove the veracity of the UFO-abduction reports, one can conclude that the test findings are *not inconsistent* with the *possibility* that reported abductions have, in fact, occurred." (Emphasis added.) The Nissensons noted that Slater's term "not inconsistent with" merely signifies that the test findings neither support the notion that UFO abductions occurred nor contradict that possibility.

The Nissensons believe that Slater offered a remarkably clear and simple evaluation of an important aspect of her test results when she noted that the characteristics that all nine subjects shared "*may* relate to *other* aspects of the subjects' lives and have *no* connection whatsoever to UFO abduction. There is really no way of knowing." (Emphasis added.)

Slater noted that the traits found among all of her subjects included "a surprising degree of inner turmoil as well as a great degree of wariness and distrust." And she added that "if one considers the skepticism and disrepute that is typically encountered with reports of UFO sightings, then not only are we characterizing UFO abduction as inherently traumatic, but we must add that it would likely carry social stigmatization as well. Moreover, assuming for the sake of argument that abduction has actually occurred and that presumably its occurrence would be very rare, it then becomes something that cannot be readily shared with others as a means of obtaining emotional support."

This erroneous presumption undoubtedly was based on what Slater had been told by Hopkins and had read in his book, and it reveals that she was unaware of the international celebrity status, and in some cases financial gain, achieved by those who claim UFO-abductions. Based on this erroneous presumption, Slater suggested that "the closest analogy might be the interpersonal alienation of the rape victim, who has been violated most brutally but somehow becomes tainted by virtue of the crime against her."

Slater concluded her addendum by saying that, "while the test findings do not rule out the possible veracity of UFO abduction, there are a number of limitations to the study which must be cited along with recommendations for further inquiry." The psychologist said that "careful interviewing of the subjects is necessary to support the conclusion that these individuals are not prone to fugue states or multiple personality configurations" despite the rarity of such mental states.

She also recommended a comparison of the test results of the nine "abductees" with those of a random sample who had not reported such experiences. Slater also noted that at least some of the nine were familiar with the subject of UFOs prior to their hypnosis sessions, "raising the possibility that their reports derive from suggestibility rather than their own buried memories." She recommended that interviews be conducted with the subjects to help determine "how prone to suggestion these subjects are."

When clinical psychologists Marc and Norma Nissenson were asked to comment on Slater's addendum report, they expressed the opinion that it contained "distinct overstatement, unfortunate oversight of important material, and a seeming failure to consider a number of statements she had made in her original report on the test findings." But they did comment favorably on Slater's "efforts to maintain intellectual integrity and professionalism in some of her closing remarks," such as those quoted above.

Professor Hines challenged Slater's assumption that abduction stories could be fantasies only if the subjects were pathological liars, paranoid schizophrenics, or otherwise seriously disturbed persons. Hines noted that "almost everyone has had dreams that, upon awakening, were so vivid that, at least for a while, it was not possible to tell if they really happened." Most people are able to sort out dream-fantasy from reality, he added. But those who seek out Hopkins to report their UFO experiences, after having read his book or seen or heard him on television or radio, clearly have a strong interest in UFOs and are inclined toward belief.

Noting that Slater found the nine subjects to be low in self-esteem and identity, Hines commented that "it is just such people that one would expect to be suggestible and leadable." When they are subjected to hypnosis by Hopkins, who "passionately believes that these events are real and uses leading questions, it is not surprising that some individuals will report, and perhaps believe, their stories of dramatic abductions."

Although FUFOR has sufficient funds to sponsor a number of modest UFO research programs and Hopkins has sufficient resources to make several visits to Indianapolis and to bring numerous subjects to New York for hypnosis sessions, neither has seen fit to sponsor the further psychological tests recommended by Slater.

Instead of asking an experienced clinical psychotherapist to review and comment on the Slater tests, FUFOR turned to sociology professor Ronald Westrum, who is on record as endorsing the extra-terrestrial UFO hypothesis. In Westrum's commentary, he claims that Slater's addendum "finds the [alien] abduction hypothesis to be consistent with her data." This is a biased interpretation of what Slater actually wrote, and omits her important qualifications. According to Westrum, "It appears that the data suggest a real traumatic experience rather than a hallucination caused by psychosis." The Nissensons comment: "There is no support whatsoever for this statement."

Dr. Slater's presumption that UFO-abduction victims, like victims of rape, "would likely carry social stigmatization" and that their stories would be something "that cannot be readily shared with others," leading to "a deep sense of shame, secretiveness and social alienation," would be shown to be false beyond any doubt in the spring of 1987, following publication of Hopkins's second book. At that time, some of Hopkins's subjects would eagerly shed their anonymity to appear on television and radio talk-show programs to tell their stories.

Twelve

Three "Victims"

Budd Hopkins often acknowledges that any single abduction tale is "totally unbelievable" by itself, but that it is the pattern of similarity of many such tales that collectively make them all credible. Even if one were to accept this Hopkins claim, there would be the critical issue of his standards for "similarity."

If an honest-to-goodness extraterrestrial visitor were to see me standing alongside the handsome and charming movie actor Robert Redford, the ET *might* logically conclude that we were quite similar: we both have two eyes, two ears, a nose, and a mouth in the same part of our face; we both have two legs and two arms with hands containing five fingers. The most notable differences an ET might observe are that I am slightly taller and have less hair, but that might seem inconsequential. However, in the eyes of a Hollywood film producer looking for a leading man for his next movie, the *differences* between us would vastly overpower these similarities. Thus, similarity, like beauty, is in the eye of the beholder.

For example, in Hopkins's book *Intruders,* he reports the dreams and/or hypnotic recall of four female subjects of seeing strange-looking babies that he believes were hybrid offspring earlier removed from their wombs. On page 185, Hopkins tells his readers that "the women's descriptions of these tiny babies are *"extraordinarily alike."* Yet only 13 pages earlier, Hopkins says the descriptions of the babies were "somewhat different [but] many of the similarities are striking."

Hopkins chooses to focus on the similarities and to disregard the significant differences. For example, one young woman described the baby's skin as being white, while another said it was grayish. Kathie Davis described the baby seen in her dreams as looking "like an old man," while attractive Andrea said the baby in her dreams "looked like me. . . . She had long, thin black hair." And still another woman described the baby as looking "like a newborn lamb. . . sort of half human."

Because Hopkins cloaks all of his subjects in anonymity to protect their privacy, it is difficult for a skeptical investigator to gain access to them for an independent appraisal of the similarities and differences in their tales. My suspicion that Hopkins emphasizes superficial similarities and disregards significant differences was confirmed when two of his subjects appeared with him on the popular Oprah Winfrey television talk-show on May 22, 1987, in which I also particiiped.

One of the "abductees" was Constance Morgan, an aspiring young actress from New York who had appeared with Hopkins on an earlier ABC-TV network show called "20/20," dealing with UFO-abductions. The other subject was a Canadian woman named Dorothy Wallis, who also had appeared on an earlier Canadian Broadcasting Company television show dealing with the same subject. Because Oprah Winfrey gave each of the two women considerable time to recount their abduction stories, almost without interruption, their tales provide useful insights into Hopkins's claimed similarities.

Constance Morgan said her abduction had occurred in November 1978, when she was living in Kansas City and was employed as an account executive at a television station there. She said it was about three o'clock on a Saturday morning when she decided to go to sleep and went to the living room of her ground-floor apartment to close the curtains at a large picture window. As she stood at the window, Morgan said, "I heard a huge helicopter noise, and it was very loud. I thought, my gosh, something must be happening. Maybe it's a police helicopter scouting for prowlers." (Her description of a very loud helicopter noise conflicts with almost all UFO sighting reports, where eyewitnesses report the UFO made absolutely no noise. This is often stressed to demonstrate that the object could not possibly have been a helicopter or fixed-wing type aircraft.)

Morgan said she looked up through the picture window at the object, about 50 feet above the ground, and said it "was *not* a helicopter. I myself did not believe my own eyes. So I made a sketch of it. . . . I told myself I'd better memorize this because nobody else is going to believe it." Her sketch, which she showed, was not the traditional saucer-shaped UFO but more dome- or egg-shaped, and she said it reminded her of a planetarium. She said the bottom of the UFO was translucent, the angular sides were a "sort of metallic color," and there was a ring around the object that was about 20 feet in diameter. "Inside this ring—don't ask me how I know this—I think I know how it works. There are metal fins, shaped at an angle, and this outer ring goes around very, very fast. It works [like] a helicopter. That's my feeling," Morgan said.

"I was afraid it might take me and so I was hiding. . . . Then I said, 'Connie, you fool, you fool. First of all, you don't believe what you're seeing. . . . [then] I said to myself, if what I'm seeing is real, then it's got to be a higher intelligence than yourself. And if that's the case, and if it wanted to harm you then it possibly could have already done so, and it hasn't. So I thought, Connie, you fool, if what you're seeing is real, and if that is a higher intelligence, then this is a chance to learn and *an opportunity of a lifetime that not the average person has,"* Morgan said.

"I stared up at this craft—and I can't explain how it happened— but *the craft got closer and closer—but the craft did not move.* What happened, some way, somehow, is that I physically went up *through the glass window,* outside and into the air. And I'm cupping my hands, like this, to try to look inside one of the [UFO] windows," Morgan recounted. Then (perhaps for the benefit of Hopkins, who was sitting next to her) she added: "I looked at the clock before I went to close the curtains. . . . It was three o'clock in the morning. . . . The next thing I remember, I found myself sitting in my bedroom, atop the covers, wide awake, clutching my knees like this . . . and terrified."

Morgan said that, although she had looked in the UFO window, "I cannot remember what I saw inside. I cannot remember." But several minutes later, in response to a question from Winfrey, Morgan seemingly forgot her recent statement that she did not remember what she had seen inside the UFO and described the creatures as being "humanoid . . . very small frame, about four to four and a half feet tall." She said their skin was "very *dark olive green, could even be mistaken for black."* (Emphasis added.)

When Morgan was asked if the UFOnauts had talked to her, she replied: "There was nothing verbal. It was all mental, telepathic." When she was asked what messages she had received telepathically, Morgan replied: "I don't remember, I'm sorry."

When Winfrey asked Dorothy Wallis if she had had a similar experience, Wallis replied: "Yes—I've had a number of experiences. My first was when I was eight years old. I woke up about 11:00 P.M. with this compulsion to go down to a nearby field. . . . When I went out of the house, the clock said 11:00. So I went down, and in this field was a very bright light, obviously shining out of a doorway. And there was this huge craft behind it—I would guess 30 feet across—and there was this little being in the doorway—very much as she [Morgan] described it. Three and a half to four feet tall, with huge compelling eyes, and he communicated that he wanted me to come in."

When Winfrey asked, "How did he communicate that, and how do you know it was a 'he'?" Wallis replied: "I don't know. I had a feeling of a man." When Winfrey asked if the UFOnaut's skin was black, as Morgan described, Wallis said: "I would call it more of a tannish gray." Continuing with her story, Wallis said: "The door closed behind me, and he asked me—there were two other beings, maybe three inches taller—and they wanted me to get up on the table. . . . They asked me to get up on this table."

When Winfrey responded: "How did they ask you?" Wallis ignored the question and continued with her story: "When I argued, they just put their hands on my arms and I was flat on my back on the table. I was absolutely unable to move. I *could move my head,* but the rest of my body was just paralyzed. They proceeded to take this scraping off the arm." Then, she reported, the UFOnauts inserted an instrument "with a 2 cm. metallic burr up into the nostril. [A 2 cm. object would be about ¾″ in diameter.] And they just sort of generally examined me all over."

When Wallis was asked about her subsequent abductions, she said the second had occurred when she was 15 and "was a daytime sighting." She explained that she and her brother were returning home from school at about 2:30 in the afternoon when they saw a flying saucer, about half a mile from where the earlier incident allegedly had occurred. She said this UFO was "a slightly different shape from the first one. And there was one being on the outside who was wearing a sort of coverall . . . and he was digging away on the other side."

Wallis said, "The same fellow who met me at the door the first time was at the door again and *he told me I would have to wait until the other one had finished what he was doing, because he could not breathe our air and that's why he was wearing a hood.*" (Wallis made no mention of what her brother was doing all this time, and Winfrey forgot to ask. Apparently he just waited patiently outside for the UFOnauts to complete their examination of his sister and made no effort to seek help to rescue her.)

According to Wallis, the UFOnauts "examined me again. . . . They checked the thing in the nostril" that allegedly had been implanted there seven years earlier. When Winfrey asked if Wallis could feel the "thing" all those years—how she knew it was there—Wallis replied, "No, I could not," and continued her story: "They inserted a long— it looked like a knitting needle—a long probe inside the navel [as reported by Betty Hill] . . . rather painful. And he told me they were taking ova—I was 15. . . . They said they were going to see if they could create a hybrid. *And that really upset me!*"

When Wallis was asked if she had ever seen her offspring or pictures, she replied: "It horrifies me. I've had dreams where I'm holding a malformed child." When Winfrey asked how Wallis knew this wasn't simply a dream, she replied: "Well, if you're using five senses, you're usually awake. And I could hear [which contradicts Morgan's claim that communications were telepathic]. I could see. I could feel. I could smell, and whatever the other one is." When Winfrey said "taste," that reminded Wallis that "they gave me a kind of blue thick stuff to drink at one point."

She continued: "When I left the craft when I was eight, he [the UFOnaut] told me I wouldn't remember, and my thought was, I will if I damn well want to." She added, "I have two-thirds recall from that strong effort," that is, without the need for hypnosis. This prompted Winfrey to ask Wallis if she had told anyone about her UFO-abductions as a child. Wallis replied: "No. My father was of a religious persuasion." She explained that her experience "had a lot of the demons in it, so I wasn't about to put myself in that."

Winfrey asked what such an experience "does to your life." "If you know it's not a dream," she said, "do you spend the rest of your days wondering if they're coming back, or why you were chosen?" Wallis replied: "Yes, you always have a sense that—they did say they would be back, that there would be things that I would be expected to do." When asked if the UFOnauts had told Wallis why they had come, she replied: "Well, they wanted the ova."

Wallis said that under hypnosis she recalled that the UFOnauts had shown her a sort of "movie" that gave her a "horrendous feeling of cataclysms on the earth, with people dying all over the place. . . . Under hypnosis I hardly looked at it. It was horrifying to me." At that point, Morgan commented that although she did not yet "have a memory of the two [missing] hours, I have the same sense that they're doing something with us involving a cataclysmic thing down the road."

Morgan challenged Winfrey's suggestion that the alleged UFO experience might only be a dream. She explained that she had the chance "to touch a [UFOnaut's] arm, and it was a very tough skin—almost lizardlike." When Winfrey asked whether this might indicate that the creatures could be "descended from lizards," before Morgan could reply Wallis commented, "I definitely had that impression."

Morgan commented that when she saw *Close Encounters of the Third Kind* (a movie dealing with UFO contact with Earthlings that was released the same year as Morgan's alleged UFO abduction), the UFOnauts shown in the movie didn't look like the beings she had seen.

The Oprah Winfrey program included a telephone call-in report from an anonymous woman who said she "wasn't actually abducted." "I kind of went aboard one on my own," she said. The incident allegedly occurred one night in 1976 when she was suffering from insomnia, and she chanced to look out the window near her bed and saw a UFO "just sitting there in the sky, about 25 feet . . . I wanted to reach over and wake my husband up and tell him, look, look at this thing that's sitting there," she said. "But I couldn't. . . . I wasn't scared. In fact, it was very peaceful.

"The next thing I knew I was standing barefoot out behind the San Antonio [Texas] airport, beside the front of my car, and the saucer was sitting there in front of me. The door opened and I walked into the ship." The woman said a voice told her to take off her nightgown and leave it near the door, which she did. Then, stark naked, she went through a passageway where she was "met by a woman that handed me a white gown kind of thing and it was very tiny but yet it covered me from head to toe."

When Winfrey asked why the woman thought she had had this experience, she replied "[I] was not the only one on the ship. . . . There were six other women from the world. There was one from Russia; there was one from South America; there was one from Canada. I was from the United States and a couple others . . . were from the larger . . . more influential countries. . . . [I] was given a bracelet that had a jewel in it and I was told that this would enable me to understand what everyone else on the ship was saying."

Then, according to the woman, "They told us that the Creator would be in in a moment. So the Creator walked in." When Winfrey asked whether this might only have been a dream, the woman replied: "I don't think it was a dream. The things that I saw I cannot really explain—the way they looked. This man [the Creator] was about seven feet tall. (Yet most UFOnauts are described as being only about four feet tall.) He told me that we were there for a purpose, that the information that we were given would not directly affect us, *but our children*. . . . We were given information which—I don't remember what it is—we were told that we would not be allowed to remember any of it until the time came."

If Hopkins found this woman's tale a bit too fanciful to believe, he did not so indicate during his subsequent comments. He volunteered that of the approximately 135 subjects with whom he has worked, there were only four or five whose stories he was unable to accept as factual.

The foregoing tales of three "abductees"—at least two of them Hopkins's subjects, whose stories he seemingly endorses—provide a benchmark by which to judge his claim that the pattern of similarity in these "incredible" stories is so impressive as to make them all believable.

One of the most incredible abduction tales is one that Hopkins would hear in February 1986, from a 40-year-old author of horror books named Whitley Strieber. Within a year, Strieber would become an international celebrity by going public with his gruesome tale in the book *Communion*, for which he was given a cash advance of $1 million by its publisher. The book would reach the top position on the *nonfiction* best-seller list of the *New York Times*, the *Washington Post*, and *Publishers Weekly*. Strieber's bizarre story will be discussed in the next chapter.

Thirteen

Communion?

In February 1986, Budd Hopkins received a telephone call from Whitley Strieber, who was eager to tell of an unusual experience that he said had occurred on the night of December 26, 1985. At their first meeting Strieber was so "very, very distraught" that Hopkins "immediately suggested that he seek some kind of therapeutic help," as Hopkins recalled during an interview on a Houston television talk-show on April 16, 1987.

Although Hopkins had by then worked with 135 subjects, all of whom he claims showed some signs of trauma because of their (alleged) experiences, he said that Strieber "was the first" he had ever suggested see a professional psychotherapist. In *Communion,* Strieber says that "Hopkins explained that he was not a therapist but could put me in touch with one if I wanted that." Hopkins suggested Dr. Donald F. Klein, director of research at the New York State Psychiatric Institute, in New York City, who would administer the four regressive-hypnosis sessions that soon followed. Klein is also professor of psychiatry at Columbia University's College of Physicians and Surgeons.

Hopkins participated in several of these sessions and thus is mentioned often in *Communion.* But, curiously, Strieber is not mentioned even once in Hopkins's *Intruders,* which he was then in the process of writing. During the April 16 Houston talk-show, when I asked Hopkins about this curious omission, he explained that Strieber's account was "rather irrelevant" for his book. Yet Hopkins said he was "thoroughly convinced that Whitley is a UFO abductee."

Strieber, by his own account in *Communion,* is a person whose life seemingly has been filled with many extraordinary, even bizarre, events. He now admits that some of these oft-told tales are not true. For example, Strieber writes: "A dozen times I have told a story of being menaced by an old college acquaintance, whose terrifying appearances and phone calls had driven us from our 76th Street walk-up [apartment in New York] to Cos Cob [Connecticut], then from there to the East 75th Street high-rise, and finally to [Greenwich] Village." Shortly thereafter he writes: "But it didn't happen; none of it happened."

Another example: When Strieber was interviewed in the early 1980s by Douglas E. Winter for his book on famous authors of horror-fiction, *Faces of Fear,* Strieber vividly described how he was almost killed by a sniper in a tower at the University of Texas in July 1966. As recounted by Strieber in Winter's book, the mad sniper "shot two girls in the stomach right behind me. And they were lying there in the grass, screaming, begging, pleading for help. . . . One was vomiting pieces of herself out of her mouth. And I could smell the blood and the odor of stomachs."

In *Communion,* Strieber admits that "for years I have told of being present when Charles Whitman went on his shooting spree from the tower in 1966. *But I wasn't there.*" (Emphasis added.) However, shortly after his book was published, Strieber again changed his story in an article written for the January/February 1987 edition of *International UFO Reporter (IUR),* published by the J. Allen Hynek Center for UFO Studies, and once again claimed that he *was* on the scene at the time of the sniper incident.

In Winter's book, Strieber described his troubled childhood: "My uncle was murdered brutally and his body left on his mother's own doorstep. My grandfather . . . died in front of my eyes in abject agony. Shortly after that, the wife of the uncle who had been murdered was burned in a fire from head to toe. . . . Shortly after that, my father . . . lost his vocal chords to cancer. . . . Right in the middle of all these catastrophes, *our house burned down.*" (Emphasis added.) But in *Communion,* Strieber admits that the house did not burn down—"Only the roof over the wing containing my bedroom" caught fire.

Strieber claims that his life has been filled with bizarre experiences, some of which he barely noted when they occurred. For example, he claims that in April 1977 he and his wife had just finished playing a phonograph record on their stereo system in their New York apartment when they heard a human voice coming over the system, as can occasionally occur due to harmonic frequencies unwittingly radiated by a "ham" radio operator or a taxi radio.

But, according to Strieber, *"the voice held a brief conversation with us,"* despite the fact that Strieber's stereo "had neither a microphone nor a cassette deck." (Emphasis added.) He says he does not remember any details of the conversation except that the mystery voice's last words were: "I know something else about you." This implies that the mystery voice had revealed knowledge about Strieber's life not generally known, which would be especially astounding. Strieber admits that, in retrospect, "I cannot understand why we didn't make more of" the incident, other than to check with someone at the Federal Communications Commission who told him that such an incident was "impossible."

In Winter's book, Strieber revealed the genesis of his book's title when he characterized himself as a "contentious, rebellious Catholic, sometimes an Episcopalian." He said: "I have been a witch. I have experimented with worshipping the earth as a goddess/mother." He also said he was a "student of Meister Eckhart, the great thirteenth-century German mystic," but that his present religious views in some respects were close to those of Zen Buddhism. Strieber notes that he spent "fifteen years involved with the Gurdjieff

Foundation," which promotes the views of a Russian "mystic."

In Strieber's article in *IUR*, he summed it up more succinctly, saying: "[I] have experimented with everything from mystical Christianity to Zen to witchcraft (of the white variety)." But he denies that he ever experimented with hallucinatory drugs as did many other college students during the mid-1960s.

According to Winter's book, between 1970 and 1977 Strieber wrote nine novels but was unable to get any of them published and earned a living working in a New York advertising agency. One night while walking in Central Park, he discovered a pack of wild dogs, which prompted him to write *The Wolfen,* a novel focusing on a pack of "werewolves" running in Manhattan. This "horror-fiction" book, published by Morrow in 1977, was an instant success and was made into a movie in 1981. His next book, *The Hunger,* dealt with vampires. His next two books, published in 1982 and 1983, dealt with the invasion of Earth by alien races and powers.

Even more significant in terms of its implications for Strieber's more recent UFO-abduction tales is his commentary on dreams in Winter's book: "There is no fear in the outside world as great as the fear that can be generated by a nightmare." While a nightmare can indeed be frightening, Strieber's extreme assessment indicates that he himself was prone to terrifying nightmares even before his alleged UFO-abduction. This could help explain his success as an author of horror stories.

Strieber, his wife, and his young son spend about half their time in a New York City apartment and the rest in a second home, which he refers to as an "isolated cabin" in upstate New York. He describes the isolated area as a "peaceful, crime-free corner of the world." Nevertheless, he had installed an elaborate burglar-alarm system, similar to one in his New York City apartment, which he is careful to activate every night before he retires.

Despite this, Strieber admits that he feels impelled in the middle of the night to search his isolated cabin, "opening closets and looking under beds . . . especially the corners and crannies." He adds: "I always looked down low in the closets, seeking something small." He admits that this obsession with possible small intruders "has been going on for a long time, although in 1985 [the year of his UFO encounter] it became much more intense." Surely this is unusual behavior for a man of 40, especially when he is living in so isolated and seemingly secure an area and has outfitted his cabin with an elaborate burglar-alarm system.

Prior to Strieber's December 26, 1985, experience, he admits that he had "read a book or two" about UFOs and that "maybe I could remember seeing something years ago in *Look* magazine about somebody named Hill being taken aboard a flying disk." Strieber's claim that he had scant interest in UFOs in recent years is challenged by the fact that his brother sent him a book dealing with UFOs as a Christmas present in 1985, shortly before his reported UFO encounter. Strieber claims that he had read no more than five or six pages of the new book prior to his December 26 experience because the book "frightened" him.

Considering that Strieber is accustomed to writing books intended to frighten their readers and that the book he was reading (by British UFOlogist Jenny Randles and astronomer Peter Warrington) is mild for this genre, his reaction is surprising. Strieber admits that the book contained a description of what he called an "archetypal abduction experience" and that he had learned of Hopkins's work with "abductees" from the book.

On the night of December 26, after an afternoon of cross-country skiing, Strieber turned on the cabin's burglar alarm, "which covers every accessible window and all the doors. . . . I made a tour of the house, peering in closets and even looking under the guest-room bed for hidden intruders." By 11:00 P.M., he and his wife were asleep in their bedroom.

Some hours later, according to Strieber, he was awakened by a "peculiar whooshing, swirling noise coming from the living room downstairs . . . as if a large number of people were moving rapidly around in the room." He reports that he checked the burglar alarm, which appeared fully operational but which had not sounded any alarm. "Then I saw . . . a compact figure. It was so distinct and yet so completely, impossibly astonishing that at first I could not understand it at all. . . . The next thing I knew, the figure came rushing into the room. I recall only blackness after that, for an unknown period of time. . . . My next conscious recollection is of being in motion. . . . Next thing I knew, I was sitting in a small sort of depression in the woods," according to Strieber's account in his book. (There is no recollection of snow, although Strieber earlier informed his readers that there were eight inches of snow on the ground near his cabin.)

In Strieber's conscious (pre-hypnosis) recollections, he described a "person . . . wearing a gray-tan body suit . . . [with] two dark eyeholes and a round smooth mouth hole," and another "working busily at something that seemed to have to do with the right side of my head . . . It wore dark-blue coveralls," he said. Later, he recalled sitting in a small circular chamber, a shape often reported by "abductees," which is not surprising considering that UFOs are reported to be circular. But, whereas others describe the interior as being spartan clean, Strieber characterized it as "messy . . . [with] some clothing thrown on the floor." This prompted him to admonish the UFOnauts: "This place is filthy."

Strieber said he recalled *four* different types of UFOnauts. The first was small and robotlike. A second type he described as "short and stocky," with deep-set eyes, pug noses, and somewhat human mouths, and wearing blue coveralls. Inside the circular room, Strieber reported seeing two more types that "did not look at all human." One of these, he said, was about five feet tall, very slender and delicate, with "mesmerizing black slanting eyes." The fourth type was somewhat smaller with black eyes that resembled buttons.

Strieber's first session with Dr. Klein must have been disappointing to Hopkins because Strieber's recollections were so rambling. He told of a UFOnaut who touched his head with a silver-tipped wandlike device, enabling him to see pictures of the world blowing up in a nuclear holocaust. He recalled that the previous November he had dreamed of seeing Cleveland destroyed by a nuclear explosion, and had recently coauthored a book with that theme called *Warday*.

Strieber comments in *Communion* that although his account of a UFOnaut "practicing psychotherapy with a fairy wand . . . is almost unique [among 'abductee' accounts], the being I saw wielding it is of a type commonly reported." During Strieber's first session, he also described disturbing recollections of his father's death, which he admits "did not reflect what really happened."

Four days later, Strieber returned to Dr. Klein for his second session and was regressed back to December 26—the day of his presumed UFO-abduction. When Strieber was asked about his state of mind in late December, he reports that he was scared and unhappy: "I felt like the world was caving in on me. Kept thinking there were these people hiding in the closet. Went through the house every night. Checking." He revealed that two months earlier he had purchased a "riot gun" for "protection." When Dr. Klein asked what he wanted protection from, Strieber replied: "Not sure. I just have the feeling sometimes . . . there are people in the house."

During this session, Strieber provided new details of the appearance of the UFOnaut that allegedly came rushing into his bedroom that night. "He looks like he's wearing cards. On his chest, this big, square blue card on his chest. An oblong one down on his middle. And he has on a—a round hat. And he's wearing a face mask with two eyeholes." But earlier in the book, Strieber mentions that the only illumination in his bedroom was that coming from a tiny pilot-light on his burglar alarm monitor, which surely would not be sufficient to see the details he described.

In addition to this UFOnaut, Strieber described many others in "blue coveralls" who marched into the room—"two rows of them." Meanwhile, Strieber's wife, Anne, remained asleep at his side, completely oblivious to what (allegedly) was occurring. According to Strieber, "They're little bitty people. I feel like I could almost pick one of them up with one hand." Despite their tiny size, they somehow transported Strieber downstairs to the front porch, where he reported seeing "a sort of black iron cot," which was used to fly him to the UFO.

When a female UFOnaut, who looked "like a person made out of leather," told Strieber that an operation would be performed on him and he realized they planned to insert a shiny thin needle into his brain, he warned them, "You'll ruin a beautiful mind." This prompted her to ask (in what Strieber said was a "startlingly Midwestern" accent): "What can we do to help you stop screaming?" Strieber responded: "You could let me smell you." When she agreed, Strieber reported "a slight scent of cardboard" which, he said, "gave me exactly what I needed, an anchor in reality."

Under hypnosis Strieber said that after the female UFOnaut agreed to let him smell her, "she drew something up from below. 'Jesus, is that your penis?' I thought it was a woman . . .—that goes right in me . . . punching in me." Despite this dreamlike sex-role contradiction, Strieber continues to refer to that particular UFOnaut as a female. At one point, he recalls that the female UFOnaut asked him "if I was as hard as I could get," and he realized he was sexually aroused. This is especially curious because he described her as "old . . . bald . . . she's got a big head and her eyes have bulges" so that her appearance reminded him of "a bug."

Later, Strieber said he was shown "an enormous and extremely ugly object . . . with a network of wires on the end . . . at least a foot long . . . and triangular in structure," which he said was inserted "into my rectum." Still under hypnosis, Strieber said he saw his now deceased father and relived a childhood train trip with his family.

Following the fourth, and last, session with Dr. Klein on March 14, Strieber reported that his nocturnal visitors returned, jabbing him on the shoulder to awaken him. According to Strieber, he could see three small people standing beside the bed, their outlines made visible by the glow of the panel on his bedside burglar alarm. He described them as stocky, dwarflike, with gray humanoid faces and glittering deep-set eyes.

Additionally, barely two feet away, was one of the thin variety, a female, with big round eyes instead of the traditional slanted eyes. According to Strieber, she appeared to be wearing "an inept cardboard imitation of a blue double-breasted suit, complete with a white triangle of handkerchief sticking out of the pocket." But when Strieber smiled at the visitors, "they dashed away with a whoosh and I was plunged almost at once back into sleep." He said he is "quite certain that the beings I saw were not a dream, and probably not a hallucination."

After his second session with Dr. Klein, on March 5, Strieber said: "[I] was doubly worried now for my sanity. First, I still felt that I might be the victim of some rare disorder. Second, I questioned my ability to live with the notion that my whole life might have proceeded according to a hidden agenda," i.e., that the many bizarre events that he believed he had experienced from his childhood might be part of a UFOnaut master plan.

Strieber added: "Neither of these alternatives was acceptable— hardly endurable—and yet one of them had to be true. . . . If I did not accept that something real was hiding deep in my life, then I had to accept myself as a disturbed man. But I did not feel or act disturbed." Strieber said that following this second session, Dr. Klein told him that "he thought I was sane." Yet later in the book, Strieber admits that after his fourth hypnosis session with Dr. Klein, on March 14, "our interest shifted . . . *to discovering some physical cause for it.*" (Emphasis added.)

Several months later, on July 26, Dr. Klein wrote a letter to Strieber "in which he mentioned that many of my symptoms were consistent with an abnormality in the temporal lobe" of the brain. Strieber explains that "people with temporal-lobe epilepsy report déjà vu, unexplained panic states, strong smells, and even a preoccupation with philosophical and cosmic concerns. They also sometimes report vivid hallucinatory journeys."

According to Dr. Barry L. Beyerstein, a psychologist in the Brain Behavior Laboratory of Canada's Simon Fraser University, persons suffering from temporal lobe epilepsy—referred to as TLEs—are characterized by "their humorlessness, excessive moral zeal, and tendency to find profound meaning in mundane events." Based on a controlled study of behavioral traits of TLEs conducted by Dr. David Bear, cited by Beyerstein, I learned that TLEs have a "penchant for somber moralization, idiosyncratic cosmological speculation, and suspiciousness toward those who question their ideas."

Further, TLEs have a "preoccupation with religious and mystical matters" and many have a history of multiple conversions from one religion to another, according to Beyerstein. He cited other studies that show that TLEs are "particularly likely to have experienced a variety of spontaneous events widely regarded as paranormal. . . . Reports of 'mystical-religious presence' were especially prevalent," he said. Also, TLEs often experience olfactory hallucinations and report a wide variety of odors.

If Dr. Klein's suspicions were correct, this would explain the many bizarre experiences Strieber recounts in his book that seemingly have plagued him since his childhood. And it would explain why Strieber could repeatedly tell extraordinary tales that he honestly believed at the time to be true, yet later would recognize were simply fantasy.

But Strieber seemingly rejected Dr. Klein's diagnosis, characterizing it as "nothing more than another speculation, essentially no different and no more supportable than the [alien] visitor hypothesis."

The week after Strieber received Dr. Klein's letter, he met a woman who claimed to be an abductee and described how "a needle with a small, knifelike handle" had been inserted in her nose. When Strieber mentioned this to Hopkins, he was told that of Hopkins's more than one hundred subjects, four (including Strieber) had reported UFOnaut "intrusions in or behind the ear, three under the eye, eleven, again including me, up the nose . . . right into the olfactory nerve with its connection to . . . the temporal lobe."

The pieces of the puzzle fit together nicely in Strieber's mind.

If UFOnauts were penetrating the brain with their nasal probes, Strieber writes, "then it may not be possible to decide between the temporaral-lobe-epilepsy and visitor hypothesis. It could easily be that the visitors are affecting the temporaral lobe in such a way as to induce abnormalities that would later be diagnosed as epileptic conditions." Yet if this were true, why did not the other ten subjects who claimed nasal probe experiences also exhibit the temporal-lobe-epilepsy symptoms noted by Dr. Klein?

Strieber did follow Dr. Klein's recommendation to undergo the painful laboratory tests designed to detect temporaral lobe epilepsy, involving the insertion of electrodes deep into the nasal cavity. Strieber claims that the analysis of the resulting temporal-lobe electro-encephalograms is "such a subjective business" that he had his own analyzed by two different neurologists, one of them a specialist recommended by Dr. Klein. (It would be more accurate to say that detection of temporal lobe epilepsy is complicated by the fact that it is a transient condition so that a single test is not necessarily conclusive.)

Strieber reports that both neurologists concluded "absolutely normal temporal-lobe function. . . . So whatever the visitors did, they did not damage me in a way detectable to our science. I am not a temporal-lobe epileptic," he said. However, this claim was contradicted by Strieber in his letter to me of May 3, 1987, in which he admitted that one of the two neurologists had not yet finished his investigation.

The appendix of *Communion* contains a statement by Dr. Klein that at first seems to give Strieber a "clean bill of health," but which on closer reading leaves a different impression. Dr. Klein's statement says he sees "no evidence of an anxiety state, mood disorder, or personality disorder." But he adds: "[Strieber] has approached the dilemma of *what is happening* to him in a careful and forthright way. . . . After an initial period of stress, he became much more calm about *his situation* and soon learned *to deal with it in a psychologically healthy way*. He appears to me to have adapted very well *to life at a high level of uncertainty.*" (Emphasis added.)

In correspondence with Dr. Klein, I learned that when Strieber called him to request a statement on his "clinical condition" for use in the book, the psychiatrist sought guidance from Strieber as to how much he should reveal and what Strieber might consider to be confidential. It was agreed that Strieber first would draft a statement indicating the range of information he was willing to reveal. Then Dr. Klein would revise the statement so it "accurately portrayed my view of his situation within the limits of his authorization." Clearly, Strieber did not invite Dr. Klein to offer a candidly complete statement.

On May 9, 1987, in my reply to Strieber's letter of May 3, I wrote: "It is my long-standing procedure, both as a journalist and an investigator of UFO cases, to seek firsthand technical expertise. In that connection, will you authorize Dr. Klein, Dr. [John] Gleidman and Dr. [Robert] Naiman to talk to me and to make full disclosures of their professional assessments of your reported experiences and the state of your physical and mental health as the latter might impact on the former?" Strieber never responded to this request.

The strongest endorsement on the jacket of *Communion* for Strieber's belief that he has been subjected to terrible indignities at the hands of strange creatures comes from Dr. Bruce S. Maccabee, a Navy physicist and longtime "UFO-believer" who heads the Fund for UFO Research, which financed Dr. Elizabeth Slater's psychological study of nine of Hopkins's subjects. (See Chapter 11.) Maccabee has had the opportunity to get to know Strieber personally as a result of being a guest on several occasions at Strieber's second home, in upstate New York.

Maccabee characterized Strieber's book as: "The gripping story of one man's repeated contact with apparent aliens or visitors. Taken in the context of the numerous similar reports which have been investigated by qualified researchers and scientists, the events so well described in *Communion* become extremely significant. Assuming that these events are factual—and I think they are—then we human beings must begin a reevaluation of ourselves and our place in the universe."

This is the appraisal of one of the UFO movement's most technically competent and rigorous investigators. It differs sharply from that of Strieber's own psychiatrist, Dr. Klein, whose assessment is based on scientific fact rather than fantasy.

Fourteen

Rivals

In the spring of 1986, as Hopkins was completing the manuscript of *Intruders,* he tried to persuade Strieber to "postpone" writing his own book about his perceived experiences. The reason, as Budd Hopkins explained during his appearance on a Houston TV talk-show on April 16, 1987, was to enable Strieber to "sort out the nightmares and fears of his discovery and what to put in the book."

Strieber chose to ignore Hopkins's advice and his publisher, Beech Tree Books (a division of William Morrow), was able to get *Communion* into the bookstores by late January, roughly two months ahead of Hopkins's new book. Sales of Strieber's book quickly zoomed and by late March it was in the number two position on the nonfiction best-seller list of both the *New York Times* and the *Washington Post,* and shortly moved up to number one. As of this writing, it has been on the national best-seller list of *Publishers Weekly* for nearly six months. This indicates that many hundreds of thousands of copies of *Communion* have been sold to date in hardcover form and millions more probably will be sold when it emerges in paperback, justifying the $1 million cash advance Strieber received.

Hopkins's book, published by Random House, was eclipsed by Strieber's success and has so far failed to make any of the best-seller lists. In an effort to overcome Strieber's head-start, Random House published a most unusual statement, signed by its publisher, Howard Kaminsky, in the form of a full-page advertisement in the *New York Times Book Review*.

Kaminsky's statement began:

> The last thing the world needs is yet another kook-book about UFOs and extraterrestrial visitations. And the last thing a quality minded publisher needs is to put its name on such a book. Those were my thoughts as I began reading *Intruders* for the first time.
>
> Four hundred and fifty manuscript pages later, I knew we had to publish this book. And, as the manuscript made its way through Random House, I began to hear my judgment echoed by some of the most brilliant, least gullible, and most savvily skeptical people I've had the pleasure to work with. Put simply, we had to publish *Intruders* because it made all of us think about extraterrestrial phenomena in a completely different way.
>
> None of us who read the manuscript *wanted* to believe in UFOs; many of us still don't . . . *totally*. Yet the events described in Budd Hopkins' manuscript—and frankly, many of them will strain your credulity almost to the breaking point—are so objectively and convincingly set down, and so compelling in themselves, that in the end, I found myself actually considering the impossible . . . that extraterrestrial visitations might, in fact, be occurring *now*.
>
> At this point you may think that both the author *and* his publisher are kooks. But it is Hopkins' calmness, objectivity and cogency—as well as the mass of medical, physical, and psychiatric evidence he presents—that make *Intruders* so *un*kooky. He is as intelligent and thoughtful as anyone I know, and questions his own evidence as severely as any skeptic would. He sympathizes·· with the doubter—but answers that the true skeptic is one who cannot deny the possibility of anything. . . .

(As I read the Kaminsky's statement, my thoughts went back twenty years to mid-November 1966, when I was weighing expressions of interest from both Random House and Doubleday to publish my first book on UFOs. I received a telephone call from Random

House's founder and chief executive officer Bennett Cerf, who sought to convince me that I should select his company.

Cerf invited me to join him and "a few friends"—including Frank Sinatra and "Mike" Cowles, whose publishing empire included *Look* magazine—for Thanksgiving dinner at his New York townhouse, and I accepted. Following dinner, Cerf assembled about 20 of the male guests and asked me to speak to them on UFOs. One of these was Cowles, who, I later learned, was favorably inclined toward UFOs and had often tried to convince Cerf. After my talk, Cerf invited Cowles to challenge my skeptical views, but he declined. Not surprisingly, Random House published my first UFO book in 1968, and a second on the same subject in 1974 prior to Cerf's death. Cerf would have been terribly embarrassed over the Random House endorsement of the Hopkins book and delighted to know that within six months Kaminsky would be replaced as second-in-command.

The first indication that relations between Strieber and Hopkins were not all "sweetness and light" came when Strieber wrote Kendrick Frazier, editor of the *Skeptical Inquirer,* a quarterly published by the Committee for the Scientific Investigation of Claims of the Paranormal (CSICOP)—an international organization of skeptical scientists, educators, and journalists. In Strieber's letter of February 1 to Frazier, he enclosed material on his just-published book, hinting that he hoped it would be reviewed in the *Skeptical Inquirer.*

Strieber's letter also mentioned that Hopkins's new book, and another on UFOs, would be published in March. He said it was terribly important that these books be reviewed in the *Skeptical Inquirer* and suggested that *he* was the logical person to write the reviews. Strieber explained that, while he considered Hopkins a friend, he disagreed with his approach because Hopkins failed to consider that some of the abduction tales might not be "entirely real."

In his letter, Strieber said that, although his book had only recently appeared in bookstores, he already had received ten letters and eight telephone calls "from people who have had experiences similar to mine." (Although Strieber did not specifically ask persons with similar experiences to contact him, as Hopkins did in both of his books, the last page of Strieber's book prominently displayed his mailing address for those wishing to write.)

Strieber concluded by stating, "I have the respect of the UFO community, and deserve it, because I have been honest and forthright with them about my experiences." He would soon be surprised, and hurt, by the UFO movement's somewhat cool reaction to his story and his book.

Budd Hopkins had long been active in MUFON, the nation's largest and most active UFO group, and had presented papers on UFO-abductions at its annual conferences in 1981, 1984, and 1985. At the 1986 conference, Hopkins received the "1985-86 MUFON Award for outstanding work in the UFO field." Strieber, on the other hand, was a newcomer and his article in the January/February 1987 issue of the *International UFO Reporter* (mailed in late April) suggested that he aspired to become the chief guru of UFO-abductions, perhaps even a spokesman for the UFO movement.

In the article, Strieber cited his appearances on more than 40 television and radio programs, including ABC-TV's popular "Good Morning America" and "The Phil Donahue Show." He said he had "taken 218 telephone calls on the air." More important, he said he had received more than 500 letters from readers of his book and was then receiving letters at the rate of 20 a day. (By May 6, when Strieber appeared on NBC-TV's popular "Tonight Show," with Johnny Carson, he reported he had received 40 letters on that day alone.)

In Strieber's article he said that 85 percent of the letters described "some sort of visitor experience." "About 40 percent report an actual abduction," he said, and added that five of the letters "appeared to be from seriously disorganized minds."

"These letters probably represent one of the largest repositories of the visitor experience ever assembled," Strieber said. He disclosed that he recently had created a nonprofit organization that would employ "professional psychologists" to catalog the reports and conduct an "extensive array of mental and physical tests" on selected volunteers. The new organization, he said, would be called the Triad Group.

(In his book, Strieber noted that he had "always been fascinated" by the triangle and that Russian mystic Gurdjieff and his disciple P. D. Oupensky put great emphasis on the triad, or triangle, as a "primary expression of the essential structure of life." During the night of February 7, 1986, while Strieber was staying in his New York apartment, he said he "felt their [UFOnaut] presence." The next morning, according to Strieber, he found "two little triangles inscribed on my left forearm.")

Strieber's article in *IUR* expressed views that would please pro-UFOlogists. For example: "For the past ten years the 'scientific debunkers' have had almost sole access to national media," Strieber claimed. Despite this, he observed, "Apparently the public simply hasn't bought a word of it. The success of *Communion* strongly suggests that the public cannot be made to believe a lie, no matter how highly placed those who promote it might be." He urged "the UFO community" to refuse to debate the skeptics, explaining that "there is no reason why people holding mainstream opinions [i.e., pro-UFO] should expect to be paired off with obvious fanatics [i.e., skeptics]."

Strieber concluded his article: "If we are to move toward the truth, it will be because the open-minded majority has found an open-minded leadership from within the UFO community. The community must have the courage to tell the truth: we don't know what is going on, but it is very real and very strange."

The May 1987 issue of the *MUFON UFO Journal* carried a rather critical analysis of *Communion* by Dr. Michael Swords, a professor of natural sciences at Western Michigan University, suggesting that Strieber's perceived experiences might be due to "internal" causes. This prompted a harsh response by Strieber, published in the same issue, in which he said: "I am increasingly becoming certain that there are large elements of the UFO community who cannot successfully address the issue of abductions in general, and my own case in particular." Strieber said:

> [I had been] warned by the other abductees before writing *Communion* that it would be dismissed by the scientists and engineers in the UFO community because it dealt primarily with the spiritual and metaphysical aspects of the experience. . . . The abduction experience is *primarily* a mystical experience, in the sense that stresses generated are similar to those created by initiation into the mystery cults of the old animist religions. And the postlude experienced by abductees . . . is usually replete with spiritual and paranormal life events. . . .
>
> I suspect that all or most of the abduction experiences as reported by UFO investigators may suffer from an unintentional fictionalization. They have been subtly altered to suggest that a quite comprehensible force is behind them. The strangeness of my account makes some UFO investigators hasten to conclude that it must represent an *internal* experience. . . .

One of Strieber's most curious statements claimed that he has "little interest in identifying the force behind the abductions." He wrote, "The issue of whether or not UFOs are real doesn't much concern me. . . . If visitors are real, *they* appear to me to be in almost total control of the situation. Therefore the search is useless because it will not bear fruit until and if *they* want it. And when *they* are ready to reveal the answer, the mystery will at once be solved." (Emphasis added.)

Such views would not endear Strieber to many in the UFO movement who get their "kicks" from investigating UFO sighting reports, speculating on such things as where the UFOnauts come from and what kind of propulsion system is used in their craft, and from being interviewed by the news media. If Strieber was correct, MUFON might as well disband and UFOlogists should find a new hobby.

Thus it is not surprising that when MUFON held its annual conference in Washington, D.C., on June 27-28, 1987, attended by more than 400 enthusiastic UFOlogists, Strieber was accorded a respectful, but cool, reception.

Two evening sessions on UFO-abductions were held on June 27. The first featured Hopkins, Dr. David Jacobs, a professor of history who recently started working with "abductees," and Indiana University professor Thomas E. Bullard, who obtained his Ph.D. in folklore and has made an analysis of about 300 abduction reports. Despite Strieber's announced plans to create an organization for UFO-abduction research, he was not invited to participate on this panel to describe his planned effort. Instead, he was one of eight "abductees" who appeared on the subsequent panel which included Charles Hickson of Pascagoula (discussed in Chapter 2).

When this second session began, Strieber was introduced by Jacobs as the author of the book that had achieved number-one best-seller status, the first time that a book on UFOs had achieved such distinction. None of the panelists had prepared remarks but responded to questions from the audience if they wished. In response to the first question about the difficulty of "going public" with the abduction stories, Strieber said he had made 225 public appearances on radio and television since January. He acknowledged that he had been paid $1 million for his book, adding that "I have cried all the way to the bank . . . but I've earned every penny of it." He revealed his hurt at being ridiculed during his appearance on the Phil Donahue show.

The following morning Strieber gave one of several dozen "contributed" papers that had been volunteered by authors, each of whom was given 15 minutes time, as distinguished from "invited" papers, such as one by Jacobs, which were allotted 30 minutes. Strieber reported that his experiences with his "visitors" during the past year had been "very unlike what happened to me before." Some of them were "so subtle" that he would have discounted them but for the presence of other witnesses. "If this isn't an experience with real visitors, then it becomes certainly the most witnessed paranormal experience I have ever heard of," Strieber said.

He also revealed plans to write a new book, detailing his more recent experiences, and explained that he has gained important insights that the public needs to know. He reported "removal of fear by confrontation with it, and eventually leading to understanding of what was happening to me to where I really don't fear any more." More important, he said, was "a response from the other side [i.e., the 'visitors'] that was intelligent and effective. . . . This was followed by what I can only describe as a period of psychological probing, which is the part that I would have personally discounted if this thread [*sic*] of witness had not been present," he added.

In *Communion,* Strieber wrote that he had "received a great deal of material about the perilous condition of the earth's atmosphere" from his "visitors," which he included in the book *Nature's End,* coauthored with James Kunetka. In March 1986, he said, he had held a press conference in Washington "to warn about the serious implications of the hole that had been detected in the ozone layer over the Antarctic. My apparent visitor information suggested this hole would lead to further holes over the Arctic and thereafter a thinning of the ozone layer over the Northern Hemisphere, with measurable crop damage from excessive ultraviolet light beginning to occur in the 1990-1993 period. At the time I gave this warning, the only stories about the hole were saying that its significance was not understood. I had also been told that the atmospheric problems will cause a reduction in immune system vitality in all animals, and the consequent resurgence of disease." Strieber admitted in *Communion* that he did not reveal to reporters at his Washington press conference that his "visitors" were the source of his predictions for fear "my credibility would be destroyed."

In Strieber's more recent MUFON conference paper, he said he had just heard from an Australian scientist that a new hole in the ozone layer over the *Arctic* had just been discovered, as he predicted, but he admitted that he had no hard confirmation. (Nor has there been any confirmation as of this writing.) He said there had been a 200-percent increase in rabies in the Northeastern part of the United States during the past two years and a comparable increase in Western Europe during the past five years, confirming his earlier prediction of damage to immune systems.

Strieber also reported that the "amount of atmospheric haze is rising, at least in my perception and . . . [according to] a friend who is a meteorologist." Strieber said the haze "is very dangerous" and that it "would spread over the Northern Hemisphere of the planet over the next three to five years rather dramatically." He admitted that he lacked the scientific background to evaluate the information provided by his "visitors," but offered to make available tape recordings he has made.

Strieber concluded by saying that "if this experience emerges in the direction that it appears it's going to, there are going to be made—not by me—some extremely controversial, startling and profoundly upsetting revelations in the next year or so. If that happens, we're going to end up with a very different view of ourselves than we have now. . . . It's going to be extremely hard. . . . We're living on a planet which is in the process of deteriorating in very unpleasant ways which we will be able to predict the outcome of but not able to affect to any great degree because of what has already gone on in the past.

"At the same time, many of the mythological underpinnings upon which we have relied for the sense and coherence of our cultures will be shaken, as well as our understanding of our own purpose and meaning in life. We could not have chosen—any of us—a more difficult time in which to be alive [or] a more challenging one. See you next year," Strieber said.

Strieber's remarks suggest that he now sees himself as a modern-day messiah who has been chosen to warn the people of this planet, bringing them not the Word of God, but of the omniscient UFOnauts.

Fifteen

UFOlogy's New Era?

Attendees at the 1987 MUFON conference in Washington, held on the fortieth anniversary of the first UFO report to achieve international attention, were told that UFOlogy had entered a new era as a direct result of the UFO-abduction phenomenon. This appraisal came from David M. Jacobs, associate professor of history at Temple University, who has served as the UFO movement's historian since publication in 1975 of his book *The UFO Controversy in America.*

This book, derived from Jacobs's Ph.D. thesis at the University of Wisconsin, offered the reader a very one-sided, pro-UFO version of the controversy. For example, although Jacobs characterized me as "rapidly becoming the new leader of the anti-UFO forces," he never once wrote or called me to obtain my views or to verify statements he planned to attribute to me, resulting in several major errors. Instead, Jacobs chose to lean heavily on the views of pro-UFOlogists, some of whom he interviewed several times.

In the book, Jacobs made only brief mention of the Betty and Barney Hill case, but said the "Hills had circumstantial evidence to bolster the credibility of their claim." He also briefly discussed the Pascagoula incident and quoted Hynek as saying he was certain that Hickson and Parker had had "a very real, frightening experience." Since 1975, Jacobs had been a passive observer/historian of the UFO movement and a frequent speaker at MUFON conferences.

As late as mid-1984, Jacobs seemed somewhat skeptical of UFO-abduction claims. For example, on August 12, 1984, at a regional MUFON conference in Massachusetts, he emphasized that UFO-abduction cases "require exceptional caution." He noted that a person making such claims may be "telling the truth, lying, or thinking he is telling the truth, but isn't." Several years earlier, Jacobs had been introduced to Hopkins by a mutual acquaintance, and by the mid-1980s they had developed a close relationship. Jacobs's views began to change as he himself acquired skills in hypnosis and began to work actively in the abduction field.

The first external indication of Jacobs's changing views came in a paper he gave at the 1986 MUFON conference, held June 27-29 in East Lansing, Michigan. Jacobs said: "In the past decade, a steadily increasing flow of abduction reports have come to the attention of UFO researchers. These reports could be, in my estimation, the most significant aspect of the UFO phenomenon since the controversy began in 1947. Like the first reports of occupants [creatures that were reportedly seen in or near a UFO], they have met with incredulity and resistance from UFO researchers anxious to disassociate themselves from bogus claims. But also like the occupant claims, their quantity, content, patterns, and the credibility of the victims are slowly forcing UFO researchers to accept them as an important element in the UFO debate."

Jacobs continued: "For the first time, researchers are given an insight into the *motivations and methodology of the intelligence behind the phenomenon.* Each case contains a wealth of detailed information, generally consistent from case to case, that was unavailable from sighting reports. . . . In their totality, abductions have the potential of being the Big Breakthrough for which UFO researchers have been waiting so long, . . . which promises . . . to fundamentally and irrevocably alter our conceptions of the UFO phenomenon forever." (Emphasis added.)

In his 1986 paper, UFOlogy's historian admitted that "before this breakthrough will be accepted by the UFO research community, the reports must be established as a legitimate part of the phenomenon." He conceded that "abduction stories are often incredible and bizarre. Some contain elements that, if they were not coming from credible victims, would appear to be extremely ludicrous and to violate common sense. . . . Presently researchers are engaging in a lively discussion about the validity of these cases."

Jacobs admitted that "sometimes psychologically ill people do claim contact with beings from other planets. These contact claims are part of their psychosis and are consistent with a whole range of bizarre thought patterns and behavior that are immediately recognizable by others, and certainly by trained psychologists." But neither Hopkins nor Jacobs is a trained psychologist. Jacobs claimed that "abduction claimants appear to have little in common"—thereby ignoring the findings of Dr. Elizabeth Slater. (See Chapter 11.)

UFOlogy's historian also chose to ignore the important lessons of the "Imaginary Abductee" experiment (see Chapter 5) and the warnings voiced by Dr. Martin T. Orne of the ease with which a hypnotist can unwittingly implant "pseudo-memories." (See Chapter 6.) Ignoring this hard evidence and its important implications, Jacobs claimed that "hypnosis would emerge as one of the most powerful keys available to unlock the mysteries of the mind."

Within a year, the metamorphosis of Jacobs would be complete. At the 1987 MUFON conference, he characterized Hopkins's new book as "monumentally important." He pronounced that "abduction research has given us more information about the UFO phenomenon itself (as opposed to the societal reactions to it) *than all the accumulated information of the last forty years. The tapping of this information has for the first time since the phenomenon began constituted an intellectual breakthrough of unimaginable and incalculable importance.*" (Emphasis added.)

For the past forty years, Jacobs said, "virtually all public debate centered on the reality or non-reality of either a specific sighting or the phenomenon as a whole, but we were unable to break into the meaning of the phenomenon. We debated about the meaning of external manifestations of an internally directed phenomenon. Doubtless this will continue, but for the first time we have developed a different set of data on which to base our knowledge and hypotheses." Jacobs concluded: "We may be on the threshold of momentous discoveries. Going through the threshold could intellectually lead us to another universe."

Little more than a decade earlier, when Jacobs was writing the fifth chapter of his book, he offered a contemptuous account of the "contactees" of the 1950s. These were persons who claimed that they communicated with UFOnauts who sometimes gave them rides on their flying saucers. In his book, Jacobs referred to them as "psychologically aberrant individuals" who claimed "to *have mystical encounters with spacemen.*" (Emphasis added.) Later in the chapter, Jacobs wrote that "the contactees' influence on the public and press hampered serious UFO researchers' efforts to legitimize the subject . . . [and] was probably the most decisive factor that prevented professional people and the public from treating the subject seriously."

In Jacobs's 1986 MUFON paper, he claimed there were important differences between contactees and abductees, noting that "contactees actively sought money and publicity [while] most abductees have sought neither." This ignores Betty Hill, Pascagoula's Hickson, Travis Walton, Betty Andreasson, Whitley Strieber, and others who seem eager to appear on radio and television talk-shows. Even Kathie Davis, the centerpiece of the Hopkins book, appeared on a Chicago television program on May 16, 1987, *using her real name of Debbie Jordan.* (The Kathie Davis pseudonym will continue to be used here to avoid confusion.) Jacobs claimed that "contactee stories were deeply rooted in a science-fiction model of alien behavior [while] abductee stories have a profoundly alien quality to them that are strikingly devoid of cultural programmatic content"—whatever that is intended to mean. He chose, for example, to ignore the claim of Connie Morgan (see Chapter 12), a Hopkins-endorsed "abductee," that she was transported through a plate glass window of her apartment to the hovering UFO in a manner similar to that employed in the popular Star Trek television series.

Jacobs said: "Abductee claims contain minute details known only to a handful of researchers. There is no possibility that the abductees would chance upon them . . . to make their claims valid." That is, *unless* they acquired them at one of Hopkins's frequent "gab-fests," where "abductees" discuss their experiences with other such subjects, or Hopkins unwittingly supplied them, possibly by his leading questions.

I was not the only one at the 1987 MUFON conference who perceived a similarity between the tales of contactees and abductees. For example, Hilary Evans, a member of the council of the British UFO Research Association (BUFORA), told me he was "shocked" by "this wholesale commitment to accept these experiences at face value." While Evans expressed admiration for Hopkins's work, he was critical because Hopkins failed to "consider the extraordinary similarity of the abduction wave to the previous contactee wave . . . which everyone now rejects." He also saw a parallel with the Middle Ages in Europe, when "many people believed in witchcraft and claimed they flew through the air to go dancing with the Devil."

Evans said that in conversations with officials of MUFON and the Fund for UFO Research he had expressed his concerns and recommended creation of a committee of qualified persons outside the UFO movement to make an independent evaluation of the abduction phenomenon. Evans characterized the tone of the evening session with a panel of eight "abductees" as "more like a religious cult than a scientific meeting."

Concerns were expressed in a contributed paper by James Melesciuc, MUFON's state director for Massachusetts, who briefly reviewed the history of abduction reports and of contactee claims. He noted a new variety, "channeling," popularized by movie actress Shirley MacLaine. Melesciuc cautioned: "Abduction casework is not for everybody, especially those members who have only very recently begun to study UFOs. Only a select group of investigators in the UFO field are truly knowledgeable in the patterns of abduction experience to decide whether or not a case has been contaminated by reading of contactee literature." He warned that failure to recognize psychotics or deliberate hoaxers "could ruin the reputation of the investigator and cause great embarrassment to the organization."

In Jacobs's 1987 MUFON paper, he claimed that tales told by subjects under hypnosis reveal the "motivation and intentions" of the UFOnauts and he did not challenge Hopkins's theory of an extraterrestrial genetic experiment. Never once in Jacobs's paper did he even mention the "imaginary abductee" experiment that had been conducted more than a decade earlier, which cast serious doubt on the validity of the data that Jacobs found so impressive. Nor was there any mention of the use of safeguards during hypnosis so strongly recommended by Dr. Orne.

Although Jacobs previously had been simply a passive observer of the UFO scene, it was clear that he was caught up in the excitement of his new, active role as an "abductionist." Jacobs said such investigations involve "delving into people's lives, into their minds, and ultimately into *extremely personal details of their lives.* . . . This is not something that just anyone can do." He added: "It is something that takes a certain set of skills. It takes a certain kind of training. It takes a certain sort of sensibility and it takes a lot of knowledge."

And what are Jacobs's own qualifications for this role? A Ph.D. in history, a deep-seated belief in extraterrestrial visitations, and a short course in hypnosis and tutelage by Budd Hopkins, who was trained as an artist. Neither Jacobs nor Hopkins has any formal training in psychotherapy. Of even greater concern, *neither seems to recognize the need for such training.*

During the evening session, in which Hopkins and Jacobs participated, Jacobs noted: "There is a tremendous danger and the danger is that everybody is going home and try it, almost as if it is a parlor game. So I would like to warn you. This is . . . serious business." He said "I give every person I interview a very, very strict warning. And my warning is that this is something . . . in them they may not even know . . . but they may feel they have seen something—something has happened to them and they are interested in finding out. . . . I tell them that the decision to find out is quite possibly the biggest decision of their life. . . . I tell them that this will be one of the few times in their lives where they will be able to say yes or no *to an absolutely life-changing situation.*

"I tell them that they will be put in a different perspective with their family, with their friends. They will have a different idea of the world. They will have a different idea of themselves. This is an extraordinarily important event. . . . Go home and talk it over with your husband or your wife." Jacobs added that two of his subjects decided not to undergo hypnosis, but he did not reveal how many decided to proceed.

Many MUFON members enjoy investigating local UFO reports, an activity that consists principally of interviewing persons who have reported a UFO sighting. Although MUFON offers a training manual for new UFO investigators, there is no "licensing examination" to assure competency. At worst, an unskilled investigator may ask leading questions or fail to write down clues that could help in finding a prosaic explanation. This is to be expected, because investigators achieve recognition for reporting seemingly inexplicable cases, not for finding prosaic explanations.

Thus the worst possible consequence of such a traditional investigation is that the subject becomes convinced that he or she was lucky enough to see an extraterrestrial craft, providing the basis for a story to be told with pleasure to friends and neighbors. There is no risk of psychological scars that could last a lifetime, as with abductees.

Jacobs's claim that "abduction research has given us more information about the UFO phenomenon . . . than all the accumulated information of the last forty years" provides strong motivation for many UFO investigators to take a short course in hypnosis so they too can perform the exciting new role of abductionist and probe deeply into the minds of their subjects.

Jacobs said that he and Hopkins now suspect that there are many as-yet-undiscovered abduction cases and that many persons who have reported "plain lights-in-the-sky night sightings" may have been abducted without any conscious knowledge of the incident. Such "nocturnal lights" represent about 85 percent of all UFO reports. Jacobs's suggestion that many persons who have reported UFOs of the nocturnal-light type may have been abducted ignores the findings of Hynek's Center for UFO Studies (CUFOS).

Allan Hendry, who served as a full-time investigator for CUFOS for several years, was able to find prosaic explanations for more than 90 percent of the nocturnal-light cases, which often turned out to be bright stars or planets. (Hendry was handicapped by the fact that he could afford to spend, on average, only a couple of hours investigating each case.)

During the 1987 MUFON session on abductions, Jacobs was asked whether the data in hand indicated that Earth was being visited by UFOnauts from different worlds. Jacobs responded that in approximately 90 percent of the cases, "similar occupants have been described," but he acknowledged that "within that similarity there are variations." The remaining 10 percent, Jacobs said, "do not match at all, and within that 10 percent they don't match [one another] at all. So we don't really know what we are dealing with in terms of the scope of the phenomenon—not the scope of the abductees but the scope of the abductors."

When Jacobs was asked if he had noted any common personality characteristics among the abductees, he replied: "I would say there are a larger percentage of people . . . that may be interested in *things paranormal.*" (Emphasis added.) But he added that he could not be sure because he did not know how many people in the general public were also especially interested in the paranormal. Jacobs said that he and Hopkins "think the [abduction] phenomenon is very widespread. . . . We are fairly certain that there are *many thousands of people [abductees]* out there at the very least." He complained of the "absolute avalanche of evidence. It is something that we cannot deal with because there are so few of us who are attempting to. . . . We have so many bits of data that we cannot assimilate it all. It's quite astounding and extraordinary."

To help them to identify potential victims, perhaps Hopkins and Jacobs should develop a parlor game called "Were You Abducted by a UFO?" which might become as popular as the game of Monopoly. At the start, a player would draw a card that asks: "Have you ever looked at your watch and been surprised to find it was an hour later than you expected? If so, draw a card from the Missing-Time pile." Or the card might read: "Have you ever started out on a several-hour automobile trip and arrived at your destination somewhat later than you originally expected? If so, draw a card from the Missing-Time pile."

A card drawn from the Missing-Time pile might read: "Have you ever had a nightmare in which you dreamed strange things happened to you? If so, draw a card from the UFO-Sighting pile." And a card drawn from the latter might read: "Have you ever seen a light in the night sky that you could not immediately and positively identify? If so, probably you are a UFO-abduction victim. Please write Budd Hopkins or David Jacobs at the following address to arrange for a hypnosis session."

It might prove to be a popular parlor game. But, in my opinion, it would be a dangerous game.

Sixteen

"Absurd" Suggestion?

Imagine that your young son was abducted from your home by a foreign terrorist group, such as Hezbollah, and was returned with a leg wound whose scar he would bear forever. And the same day you learned that a neighbor's 13-year-old daughter also had been abducted by the same terrorist group and impregnated with the sperm from one of its members. Further, you also learned that still another neighbor, a pregnant young woman, also had been abducted one night by the same terrorist group and that her unborn child had been removed from her womb without her permission. And suppose that you discovered that similar incidents, involving the same foreign terrorist group, were occurring around the nation. What would you do?

Surely you would report the incidents to local law enforcement officials, and more probably—because they occurred nationwide—you would report them to the Federal Bureau of Investigation, the U.S. government agency responsible for bringing kidnappers to justice. These are serious crimes and if a foreign terrorist group were responsible the resources of the nation would be mobilized promptly to assure the safety of our citizens.

I raised this issue during my first conversation with Budd Hopkins on April 16, 1987, when he appeared on the KTRH-TV talk-show in Houston to promote his new book and I participated by telephone from Washington. When I asked Hopkins if he had reported these alleged UFO-abduction crimes to the FBI, he replied: "That is the most absurd thing I've ever heard in my life." When I asked Hopkins, "If I abducted you or a member of your family, would you report it to the FBI," he replied, "I certainly would." I responded, "Then why don't you report these alleged abductions to the FBI?" Hopkins replied, "Phil, that is so patently absurd," and he refused to discuss it further.

When Hopkins was interviewed subsequently by Dave Matheny, a staff writer for the *Minneapolis Star and Tribune,* for an article published in that newspaper's April 28 edition, he said that his book already was into its second printing although its first run of 62,500 copies "only hit the bookstores this month." When Hopkins was asked whether UFO-abductions should be reported to the FBI, his quoted response was: "This is the bizarre Philip Klass thing. . . . Nobody is going to report this to the FBI. It's like trying to report it to the EPA [Environmental Protection Agency]. It's totally irrelevant. . . . I think Klass is a despicable human being because he's trying to discredit the witnesses."

Not at all. I simply wanted an independent FBI investigation of Hopkins's claims, knowing that if they were confirmed President Reagan would certainly take appropriate action to halt such indignities against U.S. citizens, as evidenced by his concern and action to recover hostages abducted by foreign terrorist groups. And if an independent FBI investigation showed that UFO-abductions were simply fantasy, it would end needless public concern.

Several days after Hopkins first rejected my suggestion, I received a telephone call from Paul Kurtz, chairman of the Committee for the Scientific Investigation of Claims of the Paranormal (CSICOP). Kurtz expressed his serious concern for the public's peace of mind because of UFO-abduction fears generated by Strieber's and Hopkins's book promotion campaigns on television and other news media. He was especially concerned because of Hopkins's claim that UFOnauts abduct young children and perform surgical experiments on them.

Based on my 21 years of experience in investigating prominent cases, all of which proved to have prosaic explanations, I told Kurtz I was sufficiently confident to risk personal bankruptcy to demonstrate that the public need have no UFO-abduction concerns. As a result, CSICOP issued a press release in which I offered to pay any "victim" $10,000, "providing the alleged abduction is reported to the Federal Bureau of Investigation and FBI investigation confirms that the kidnapping really occurred." But the press release cautioned that "anyone who knowingly reports a spurious kidnapping to the FBI is vulnerable to a $10,000 fine and up to five years in prison."

On May 10, I wrote Hopkins, enclosing a copy of the press release. My letter asked that he inform his many dozens of "victims" of my offer "so that any who wish can avail themselves of this opportunity." My letter concluded: "I would hope that those of you who claim to have evidence of 'UFO abductions' will promptly submit it to the federal authorities so that it can be investigated and either confirmed or refuted. Either of these alternative conclusions would be a great service not only to your fellow citizens but to all residents of this planet."

(While there is sharp disagreement over how effective President Reagan's proposed "Star Wars" program might be in defending against a massive Soviet ballistic-missile attack, there is no doubt that the United States could promptly deploy powerful ground-based free-electron lasers that could easily "zap" a handful of incoming UFOs. If Hopkins's evidence of a "UFO-abduction" threat is as convincing as he claims, surely Congress would join the president in pressing for rapid deployment of a "Star Wars" system to protect the nation's citizens against UFO intrusions. And the president could offer the technology to other friendly nations to protect their people against UFO-committed crimes.)

On May 22, when Hopkins and I appeared together in Chicago

on the Oprah Winfrey show, he seemed to have changed his mind and disclosed that he had written to the FBI three days earlier. He handed me a copy of his letter, and later gave me permission to publish it. The letter is reproduced below in the format of the original. [Note: The New York address shown is Hopkins's apartment. No address was shown for the FBI to indicate whether the letter had been sent to its New York bureau or to Washington headquarters.]

246 W. 16th St.
New York, N.Y. 10011
May 19, 1987

To the Acting Director, Federal Bureau of Investigation

I am enclosing a copy of *Intruders,* recently published by Random House. My book deals with UFO abduction reports which I have collected and investigated over the past twelve years. Previously this kind of abduction case has been reported to the F.B.I., NASA [National Aeronautics and Space Administration], various local law enforcement agencies, and such military organizations as the U.S. Army and the Air Force. [Note: I challenge the accuracy of this claim.]

According to government documents made public through F.O.I.A. [Freedom of Information Act] requests, it is a matter of public record that over the past few years UFO cases have been investigated by such agencies as the D.I.A. [Defense Intelligence Agency], the N.S.A. [National Security Agency], the Air Force and other official bodies. I am writing this letter and enclosing my book for a specific purpose: to report these events to you and to ask that the F.B.I. joins [*sic*] in their investigation. If you do not feel that these cases fall within your jurisdiction I would like to be so informed, and I would appreciate being told to which agency I should address my request.

My investigation of these accounts, involving some 141 individuals, has made extensive use of psychological testing and interviewing by professional medical and psychological personnel. These medical consultants say there is no doubt that the people they have dealt with have suffered rather severe traumas, and are bearing deep psychological scars. [Note: This is a serious distortion of Dr. Slater's stated views.] Unfortunately, a few publicity-minded individuals, under the banner of "aggressive skepticism," have created an atmosphere of ridicule around anyone describing such a traumatic UFO encounter. According to these "skeptics'" complex beliefs, such an event is absolutely impossible; therefore anyone reporting such an event is by default either a liar or somehow mentally deranged. One recognizes this cruel tactic from the classic male defense in rape cases, in which the victim must of necessity be either a liar or a seducer.

My desire to protect those describing such UFO abductions has forced me to adopt pseudonyms in my book. However, if your Bureau wishes to investigate these reports a number of abductees will cooperate fully with your special agents, as will I. *Though these accounts describe anything but a conventional federal crime,* I believe the evidence is truly compelling that the experiences are real, are chilling, and literally demand to be looked into by some official government body. [Emphasis added.]

> Sincerely
> (signed)
> Budd Hopkins

During an off-the-air commercial break in the Oprah Winfrey Show, following mention of my offer to pay $10,000 to any FBI-confirmed UFO-abductee, Hopkins announced that he would pay $20,000 to any FBI-confirmed UFO-abduction victim. In view of Hopkins's claim that he is convinced that more than a hundred of his subjects are "abductees," his offer indicates either that he is eager to pay out several million dollars, or that he very much doubts that an FBI investigation will confirm his claims.

Immediately following the television show, Hopkins and I had a brief conversation outside the studio (which I tape-recorded) that went as follows:

KLASS: You have said, and I agree, that if this is true it is the biggest story of all time. I would go further and say it is the biggest threat to the people of the United States since this country was created.

HOPKINS: You really think that the idea of the UFO phenomena is that dangerous?

KLASS: No, the abductions, the alleged abductions. In other words, if American citizens are not free to drive down the highways, to retire to their bedrooms without fear of abduction.

HOPKINS: I agree, that's an awful thing.

KLASS: It is a terrible thing.

HOPKINS: I agree with you.

Hopkins tried to explain why he had never before contacted the FBI: "I've always assumed that the FBI read and listened in on radio broadcasts that people make, and television broadcasts. I had published an article [on abductions] in *Village Voice*. I've done a book [on abductions] before. And I've done this book. I assumed that the FBI would be aware that this thing is out there. You must assume that nobody in the FBI reads. . . . But you chided me so I decided to send them the goddamned book and say please read it. . . ." Hopkins added that his wife had called the FBI and said, "What should be done about these cases?"

I asked when she had called and Hopkins said, "Recently." When I asked if she had called FBI headquarters in Washington or the FBI's New York office, Hopkins replied: "You're quibbling. You're quibbling. You're quibbling." Thinking that Hopkins misunderstood my question, I repeated it and he replied: "You know what you said, you steered me toward the FBI and I said, here's the letter [May 19 to FBI], and you say, 'Why did you wait that long,' and I say well—" I interrupted to say "No, Budd, Budd," but he continued: "Now I say I reported on the telephone and you say well who did you talk to. You make a hoop and see if I'll jump through it, and I won't, I tell you."

Seeking to calm Hopkins, I said, "Budd, you just made the

statement that your wife had called the FBI," and Hopkins interrupted to say, "Yes, and aren't you pleased?" I continued: "And I simply asked [whether it was] New York City FBI or [Washington] headquarters."

Hopkins responded: "But you said the headquarters. Now you make a little hoop here and, and you say . . ." I tried to explain: "I'm simply asking questions as a UFO investigator [should]. . . ." At that point, our conversation was briefly interrupted by a member of the television studio audience.

Then Hopkins said: "The FBI thing was such a false issue . . . because these things have been reported to the FBI." Because his claim conflicted with information I had earlier obtained from the FBI, I asked him, "When?" Hopkins responded, "You know you have an interesting way of asking questions that don't have an answer." I replied: "You made a statement and when I ask you for specifics, Budd, you then . . . When have abductions been reported to the FBI?" At that point, Hopkins turned away and began to whistle.

When I pressed him for an answer, Hopkins responded: "Are you finished? Are you going to be quiet?" I asked if he was "going to answer my question," and he again replied: "Are you going to be quiet?" Shortly afterward Hopkins told me that I would receive a letter from UFOlogist Larry Bryant that would answer my question, and then he walked away, ending our conversation. I never received the promised letter from Bryant.

Later, when I studied Hopkins's letter to the FBI it struck me as a terribly casual way to alert top FBI officials to what could be the gravest threat to the well-being of U.S. citizens in the nation's history—if abductions are fact and not fantasy. I wondered if this reflected his concern over the severe legal penalties for reporting a spurious abduction to the FBI. Or was it possible that Hopkins hoped that his casually written letter would fail to motivate an FBI investigation so that he could later claim the FBI had ignored his report.

Shortly after my encounter with Hopkins, I learned that Dr.

Leo Sprinkle, the University of Wyoming psychologist who had been a pioneer in UFO-abduction research, now believed that he himself had been abducted as a young child, according to an article in the June 22, 1987, issue of the *National Enquirer*. When I wrote to Sprinkle to check the accuracy of the story, he confirmed the quotations attributed to him, but said the discovery of his own abduction under hypnosis had occurred in 1980, and not "recently" as the tabloid article reported. Sprinkle said that as a child of about ten he used to have nightmares in which he dreamed that he was standing by a table and a *tall* man was walking toward him. When he awakened, he said he had "a feeling I had been taken from bed and returned." But later Sprinkle said he had dismissed the nightmares as the product of "an overactive imagination." Sprinkle later became very much interested in UFOs, as a result of two sightings of his own. Then, in 1980, as a result of his own work in the UFO-abduction field, Sprinkle decided to ask a colleague to hypnotically regress him back to age ten. The results were interesting.

"Under hypnosis, I felt I was standing at a large window, looking out at a black sky full of stars that seemed to be moving toward me," according to Sprinkle. "I was on board some type of spacecraft with curved walls. I felt a hand on my right shoulder and an arm at the back of my neck. I looked up and saw *a very tall man. . . . He was over six feet tall.* [Recall that UFOnauts typically are said to be only about four feet tall.] The man seemed to have a human face. He was the same man I saw in my nightmares. He seemed authoritative *but also appeared gentle."* (Emphasis added.)

Sprinkle said that the tall UFOnaut spoke to him, saying: "You can help other people learn more about their purpose in life. Learn to read and write well. When you grow up, you can help them." Sprinkle said that as he "heard those words, I felt like a tremendous burden had been placed on me. But I also felt joyful. I feel like a messenger boy. I think I was taken aboard the UFO on more than one occasion—and I think those contacts were all to prepare me for my UFO research."

Is it simply coincidence that the gentle and kindly UFOnaut that Sprinkle described had a personality similar to his own? (Despite my very basic differences with Sprinkle on UFOs, our relations have always been friendly and cordial, unlike my relations with Hopkins.) Sprinkle has never reported that any of his subjects claimed to have been impregnated by UFOnauts, or to have had unborn children removed from their womb. Sprinkle's subjects typically characterize their abductors as kind and gentle, and view themselves as "cosmic citizens" as a result of their alleged experiences.

Is it possible that two basically different types of UFOnauts are visiting earth—a warm, gentle type whose victims later seek out Sprinkle, and a more cruel breed whose victims seek counsel from Hopkins? If so, how would each type of UFOnaut know in advance which victims would seek counsel from Sprinkle, and which from Hopkins?

Or is it possible that the character of the alleged experience that emerges under hypnosis reflects not only the personal UFO beliefs of the abductionist who is serving as the hypnotist and/or principal interrogator but also some elements of his personality as well? I admit that this is pure speculation on my part. But I recalled that Sprinkle works on a state university campus in a quiet, modest-size western town with few crimes of violence. Hopkins lives in quite a different environment in New York City, where the pace of living is much more frantic and where crimes of violence are much more commonplace.

At the 1987 MUFON conference, Hopkins said he had "never found details in any [abduction] report" to indicate that the UFOnauts are "malevolent." He explained, "That is, nobody has had their arm twisted, or anything like that." I can conceive of no more malevolent act than removing a flesh sample from a young child that would leave a life-long scar, impregnating a 13-year-old girl without her permission, or removing a woman's unborn child. Hopkins's stated view of what is, and is not, malevolent may explain why he took no steps for more than a decade to alert the federal government to try to halt this "invisible epidemic" until I chided him into doing so in the spring of 1987.

When Hopkins presented a paper on UFO-abductions at the 1985 MUFON conference in St. Louis, he explained that he did not want his audience "to assume that I feel UFO abductions are crimes, or that these strange humanoid abductors are evil. For all we know the UFO phenomenon may be ultimately benign. I do feel, however, that the abduction experience is—for the abductee—traumatic, and in the short term at least, psychologically harmful, but then so is major life-saving surgery traumatic and psychologically scarring." A curious analogy.

While Hopkins has convinced himself and tries to convince many of his subjects, albeit unwittingly, that they have been abducted by UFOs, if the FBI is sufficiently impressed with the evidence he offers to launch an investigation, I predict the agency will discover that some of Hopkins's subjects do not share his conviction that they have been abducted by UFOnauts. Even Kathie Davis, the centerpiece of Hopkins's book *Intruders,* has serious doubts, as she candidly revealed during the 1987 MUFON conference "abductee" symposium, to be discussed in the next chapter.

Seventeen

The "Victims" Speak

MUFON's 1987 conference, in Washington, provided the unique opportunity to see and hear eight "UFO victims"—the largest number assembled in one spot, except in Budd Hopkins's New York City apartment, where a UFO-skeptic like myself is not likely to be invited. Several of the panelists had appeared earlier on national or local television talk-shows.

Whitley Strieber was the best known of the four male panelists, thanks to his many television appearances. At least some UFOlogists present recognized another panelist, Charlie Hickson, of Pascagoula, who had acquired a mustache since he appeared on television network-news programs and numerous talk-shows in the fall of 1973, following his claim of abduction. (See Chapter 2.) Another of the male panelists was Michael Shea, a personable Washington-area lawyer, probably in his early forties, who had appeared with Hopkins on the CBS-TV "Night Watch" late-late-night talk-show two months earlier. The fourth male panelist was Peter Robbins, age 40, a soft-spoken but intense New York City artist who teaches painting.

The four female panelists included Kathie Davis, the principal subject in Hopkins's latest book, and Kris Florence, a dancer-choreographer in her early twenties who had appeared with Hopkins on ABC-TV's "20/20" program dealing with UFO-abductions, which aired on May 14, 1987. The other two female panelists were Rosemary Osnato, a woman who appeared to be in her early thirties, and a young woman in her twenties who was introduced as Susan Taylor, which chairman David Jacobs later told me was a pseudonym.

Judging from the panelists' responses to generalized questions posed by Jacobs and other questions from the audience, *none* of them could be characterized as "kooks" or "crackpots." Although the panelists knew that nearly all of those in the audience were strongly pro-UFO, most seemed reluctant to talk or to discuss their alleged experiences, except for Shea, Osnato, and Strieber, whose commentaries dominated the session. (See Chapter 14.)

If the mood of the panelists could be characterized in a single word, it would be "tense." I recalled the comment by Professor Westrum in the FUFOR report on Dr. Slater's psychological tests (see Chapter 11): "The experience . . . continues to affect the witness's life after the fact. The abductee is likely to experience unexplained fear, anxiety, phobias, nightmares, flashbacks, and quasi-memories."

I also recalled Westrum's claim that "many of these ill-effects can be helped by simply talking the experience over with a UFOlogist, although even more symptoms can be alleviated through hypnotherapy." If hypnotherapy by Hopkins and Jacobs had provided alleviation for any of the MUFON panelists, it was not readily apparent.

My own impressions were aptly summed up the following day by Hilary Evans, of the British UFO Research Association (BUFORA): "If we knew the previous history of these people, if we could explore their life situations, we would find that there was some basis that provides the need to have this kind of experience. They are all people who for reasons of their own are having psychological experiences which are accomplishing something that they need to have happen."

Evans's sage assessment reminded me of the unusual UFO-abduction tale reported by a young Phoenix, Arizona, housewife named Christy Dennis at Leo Sprinkle's 1981 conference for "abductees," held May 23 in Laramie, Wyoming. Under hypnosis administered by Sprinkle, Dennis had described her abductors as being eight feet tall and having golden hair, olive-bronze skin, and "perfect features." Even more extraordinary, under hypnosis she told of having been "transferred" to the UFOnauts' own planet.

As a result of her story and her appearance at Sprinkle's conference, the previously unknown housewife was the subject of a feature story in the December 15, 1981, issue of the *National Enquirer*. The article quoted Sprinkle as saying: "This is one of the most remarkable abduction cases I've come across."

In November 1982, Dennis visited a "therapy center" for UFO-abduction victims that had been established in Laramie by Dan Edwards and his wife, intended to "help people" who believed they had been abducted. (Edwards later admitted to me that neither he nor his wife had any formal training in psychotherapy and said he previously had worked as a quality-assurance inspector for a company he refused to identify.) During Christy Dennis's several visits to the Edwards' center, she underwent regressive hypnosis in which she described her visit to the UFOnauts' home planet. Edwards later told me that he, like Sprinkle, accepted her tale as fact because it was told under hypnosis.

Shortly afterwards, in early 1983, Dennis recanted her abduction tale in a letter she sent to Sprinkle, and to several UFO organizations, which he promptly made public. As Dennis briefly explained in the letter to Sprinkle, and later expanded on in several telephone conversations with me, she was very much concerned about the nuclear arms race and the possible destruction of the human race in a thermonuclear war. But when she voiced such concerns to friends and neighbors, their typical response was: "What makes you think you are so much smarter than our government leaders in Washington?"

So she conceived the idea of claiming that she had been abducted by UFOnauts from a very advanced civilization, whose wise leaders would tell her of *their* concerns about the future of the human race on Earth. This would enable her to express her own concerns in the words of the very wise leaders from a more advanced extraterrestrial civilization, to whom she felt her friends would give greater credence.

But these hopes were dashed, Dennis explained to me, because her friends and neighbors were much more interested in learning about the UFOnauts' lifestyle in their distant world than in "their message for Earthlings."

Still, it was not easy to admit that the abduction tale was a hoax, especially because she had been contacted by a New York literary agent who had encouraged her to write a book about her experiences, which she had done. Dennis said the agent spoke of the possibility that her book might lead to a movie that "would be as good as *E.T.*"

The necessary motivation to admit it was all a hoax finally came, Dennis told me, as a result of her last visit to the Edwards' "therapy center" in early 1983. She told me: "I realized just what kind of a messed-up life you can get if you continue with these things." She earlier had volunteered to me that she had had "emotional problems" for which she had sought professional help.

Dennis's decision to admit that her UFO-abduction was a hoax not only cost her the opportunity to supplement her family's meager finances with income from the hoped-for book and movie, but many of her new-found friends with strong interests in UFOs now treated her "as if I had leprosy," she told me. "What happens is that people identify with what you say because somewhere along the line it touches something psychological in nature and they feel a need to identify with it," she added.

She told me that she still believes some UFOs are extraterrestrial craft but expressed the opinion that many claims of UFO abductions represent simply "unrealized dreams and aspirations. And the only way they can get any kind of satisfaction is to fabricate some sort of story to get the focus of attention that they need."

This profound observation from a young woman with only modest education echoed the assessment voiced by Hilary Evans following the MUFON conference panel. But neither considered the possible "psychological needs" of abductionists like Hopkins and Jacobs, who seem to revel in the discovery of new "victims."

Sprinkle's reaction to the Dennis admission of a hoax, expressed in his memo of February 3, 1983, which made public her confession, offers useful insights into those who claim that experienced abductionists can readily spot a hoaxer. Sprinkle wrote that he was puzzled by her confession, noting that "she demonstrates in her behavior some of the characteristics of UFO contactees, including a concern about our planetary plight, and a certainty that, at various levels of 'reality,' intelligent beings are developing a wider interface with human society."

Especially surprising, considering that Sprinkle is a trained psychologist, was his statement that "I do not know of a simple psychological explanation for the complex information [on what she saw when she allegedly visited the UFOnauts' planet] which she has provided." The explanation is that, because no Earthling has ever visited an extraterrestrial civilization and returned to describe the experience, the most experienced abductionist has no criteria for discriminating between fact and fantasy.

Christy Dennis had demonstrated the validity of psychiatrist Martin Orne's contention that it is all but impossible even for an experienced hypnotist to determine whether a subject is under hypnosis or when a subject is lying. Dennis also had demonstrated how easy it is, without any significant research, to fool an experienced abductionist who is eager to believe, simply by drawing on fantasy and information acquired casually by reading UFO books and watching science-fiction movies.

Returning to the MUFON conference, it is unlikely that even a trained psychotherapist could accurately determine the possible "psychological needs" of those who appeared on the panel, based solely on their typically cautious and brief statements during the roughly hour-long evening session. Both Hopkins and Jacobs use pseudonyms for their subjects on the grounds that this will protect their privacy, which is understandable.

However, pseudonyms also make it extremely difficult for a skeptical investigator to interview these subjects and gain independent insights uncontaminated by Hopkins's and Jacobs's own strong biases. The MUFON symposium thus offered me a rare opportunity, as did the television appearances of some of the same panelists.

One of the MUFON panelists was Kris Florence, the young dancer-choreographer referred to as "Pam" in Hopkins's book. She first appeared under her real name on the ABC-TV show "20/20." As Hopkins described her experience in his book, Kris and her sister, when they were teenagers, had been driving with their mother in California when their car broke down. While the mother went for help, leaving the two girls in the car, they had experienced what Hopkins calls "an interesting missing-time experience," which he does not describe. Under regressive hypnosis, Kris "described a low, silver-gray vehicle arriving and at some point she is inside a round space." Also while she was under hypnosis, according to Hopkins, a tale emerged of an abduction that occurred when she was only five years old.

In 1979, while living with her husband in New Mexico, she found herself "accidentally pregnant" and had an abortion, and Hopkins claims that her doctor reported finding "no sign of fetal tissue." (It is surprising that a doctor would perform an abortion without a prior examination.) Naturally, this prompted Hopkins to suspect that UFOnauts had removed the unborn child.

When Hopkins asked if Kris had had any unusual dreams, she reported recurring dreams of being in an unfamiliar setting and seeing a small "half-human" baby on the floor. These dreams, hardly surprising for a woman who has had an abortion, served to convince Hopkins that the fetus had indeed been removed by UFOnauts, transplanted to a female extraterrestrial, and later shown to Kris.

But when Kris appeared on ABC-TV, she said that her only

conscious recollections were of having seen a silvery UFO a decade earlier: "That's all I can say really happened." She added that "under hypnosis, other things came out which indicate that *maybe* some sort of person or people from another world came and took my sister and I and sort of looked us over and did a few experiments."

Commenting on Hopkins's interpretation of her dreams of seeing a tiny baby as indicating an extraterrestrial genetic experiment, Kris said: "If Budd wants to conclude that, if people reading Budd's book feel that's conclusive then that's [indistinct]. *But I myself do not want to believe any of this has any connection.*" (Emphasis added.)

Kris was one of the less talkative panelists at the MUFON conference. But in response to the question of how their experiences had altered their lives, Kris said it raised grave concern over "what's going to happen to your children, and your children's children." Recall that Hopkins believes that UFOnauts select families for genetic experiments and remove flesh samples from successive generations of young children.

Strieber seemed to endorse Hopkins's hypothesis based on about a thousand letters he said he had received, "which may begin to give us some answers as to why people are selected. I think that genetics plays a role in it. I suspect . . . it happens to family groups."

Kris said that while she did not yet have any children she worried about "what's going to happen when I do—after this experience." Her comment prompted lawyer Michael Shea to express concern for his own five-year-old daughter. Later, Shea said that he frequently looks at his young daughter's legs, hoping he will not discover evidence that she has had a flesh sample removed by UFOnauts. He added jokingly, "It's not a healthy thing, you know, to look at your own daughter's legs all the time."

When Shea was interviewed on CBS-TV's "Night Watch" program, he emphasized that he was *not* convinced that he had been abducted by a UFO. Shea said that in the early 1970s, after serving in the armed forces in Vietnam, he had been driving near Baltimore when he saw a large, glowing UFO with alternating red and yellow lights. "It came towards me at very low altitude. I became very afraid. And I don't remember anything after that. . . . I get to my destination [and] I'm two hours late. There's no explanation for it."

In 1985, more than a decade after the reported incident, Shea said that after reading Hopkins's first book, *Missing Time,* he made arrangements to visit Hopkins for regressive hypnosis. Since then, Shea said, he has undergone a dozen hypnosis sessions with Hopkins and, as a result, Hopkins now believes that he has been involved in approximately 20 UFO-abduction incidents, the first of which occurred when he was only seven years old.

When the host asked if Shea really believed he had been abducted by a UFO, he replied: "I do not really believe the abduction. . . . I do not believe the abduction, but I do not disbelieve." Later, Shea added: "I could not categorically say it did not happen. It's more real than unreal. But I'm not sitting here telling you it's real. . . . I just don't believe it."

As I listened to Shea on the CBS program, I could not help but recall Dr. Orne's warnings, based on experimental evidence, about pseudo-memories, implanted intentionally or unwittingly by a hypnotist: "The pseudo-memory will have become part of his conscious memory. . . . The more frequently the subject reports the event, the more firmly established the pseudo-memory will tend to become."

For "Susan Taylor," an attractive young woman in her twenties, the MUFON symposium was her first public exposure, and she said relatively little. She did comment that "when you first realize that you have to face the reality that you've had an abduction experience, it's very terrifying."

The much more talkative Rosemary Osnato was very critical of the attitudes she said were displayed by her UFOnaut abductors: "They use a lot of tricks. They are deceitful. They lie. . . . That not only makes you angry but makes you concerned for the future. If they don't give you answers that you can expect, and maybe they're not giving you answers because you *won't* accept them, and that's what is bothering me. I don't like the idea that I'm not getting an answer . . ."

Peter Robbins, the art teacher, stressed that to the best of his knowledge he was "not an abductee," but that 26 years earlier, at age 14, he had been "zapped by a blue light from a UFO and knocked unconscious." He added that his younger sister, then age 12, who was with him, had been abducted at that time and several additional times.

Clearly Robbins viewed himself more in the role of a UFO-abduction researcher than as a victim and said he had "been very fortunate to work with some of the finest researchers in the field the past twelve and a half years—Budd [Hopkins] and Pete Mazzola." (Mazzola, who died of a brain tumor in 1987, was a member of the New York Police Department and an ardent UFOlogist.)

My chance meeting and interview with Robbins the next day, and a lengthy telephone interview a month later, on July 25, provided additional details on his claimed experience and his views on the UFO-abduction phenomenon. During our first interview, on June 28, Robbins acknowledged that "there is a percentage of people ['abductees'] who want to be talk-show personalities and write best-selling books." But he added that he knew about 25 people who he believed "have had these experiences. That something phenomeno-logically real is impacting on them. And it's not some Jungian projection of collective mythology or just wanting to be part of something bigger than yourself."

During our June 28 interview, Robbins told me that for 13 years he "didn't remember" having been zapped by a UFO. Then, at age 27, when he was just beginning to teach painting at the New York School of Visual Arts and had just moved into a loft apartment in New York's Chinatown, "for no reason I could pin down I found myself sitting on the floor of my home and starting to cry, and then I started to sob . . . and over the next 20 minutes or half an hour, like a literal tidal wave of memories . . . the thing came out bright and clear as Kodacolor film"—the memories of the UFO experience returned.

At that point our conversation ended because we both wanted to attend a MUFON session then starting, and it was not until nearly a month later that I was able to hear Robbins describe his claimed UFO experience. "At the age of 14, I looked up into the sky and there, coming at a very high rate of speed, observed by my sister as well, were five silvery white disc-shaped metallic objects. . . . They were close enough to make out yellow glowing windows around the edge. They were in a perfect military V-formation. They stopped . . . several thousand feet over a neighbor's house. Clear as a bell. . . . And as I became frightened and began to run, a blue ray of light shot out from one of them. Everything went blue. Then everything went black. I passed out in what I can only describe as slow motion," Robbins said.

"When I woke up, I had a terrible scrape on my right arm from hitting the concrete . . . and my sister was terribly disoriented and refused to talk," which many years later would prompt Robbins to conclude that she had been abducted while he was unconscious. Robbins said he and his 12-year-old sister agreed not to reveal the incident to their parents, or even to talk about it themselves.

Robbins said that, although he had not previously read any books about UFOs, following the zapping incident he felt "compelled" to visit the library to check out three books on UFOs. One was a book by George Adamski, describing his numerous flights aboard a flying saucer, including a visit to the backside of the moon where he claimed to have seen mountains covered with trees and snow. Another was a book by Donald Keyhoe, the first writer to popularize UFOs. Robbins did not remember the author or title of the third book. He said he did not read them but only "flipped through" them that night, adding that he "became even more anxious at that point. I just wanted to forget what I had seen."

(Although I did not challenge Robbins's claim that he did not read the three books he had brought home, it struck me as odd that he would not have searched them for other such UFO-zapping incidents. At the time, in 1961, there had been only one—to my knowledge—and it proved to be a hoax. In late 1975, Travis Walton would also claim to have been zapped by a UFO. [See Chapter 3.] As with Robbins, there were no burn-marks or serious injuries to support the claim.)

Robbins explained: "I knew in my heart that talking about having seen flying saucers in the sky and being knocked out by one would essentially make me a pariah [among his teenage friends]. And I resolved—because this was all too fantastic—I couldn't have seen it. Therefore I didn't see it. Therefore I had better forget it." Robbins claims he was able to completely erase all conscious memories of the extraordinary incident. However, "it caused disturbances all through the next 13 years of my life in subtle and not-so-subtle ways." Earlier Robbins had mentioned that he had undergone psychotherapy.

When the UFO-zapping memories returned 13 years later, Robbins told me, he called his sister and said: "The thing I want to talk about is terribly important. It happened to us in childhood. We've never spoken about it. I'm afraid that if I tell you even the slightest detail, you'll simply agree and I'll never know for sure if you remember what I remember." Robbins told me his sister interrupted to say she knew exactly what he was referring to and she "proceeded to tell me that exact event, including what she remembered beyond what I hadn't."

Because Robbins's claimed experience occurred in June 1961, I expressed surprise that the nationwide news media coverage given to the Hill "UFO-abduction" case in 1966 had not served to jog his memory of his own encounter. Robbins replied: "I never read [about] it. I never read a UFO book in my life." When I reminded him that *Look* magazine's articles on the Hill case were widely quoted in many newspapers, Robbins responded: "I have never had any interest in flying saucers, in extraterrestrial visitations, in any of this stuff until the memory reemerged."

Robbins said he had undergone regressive hypnosis several times by UFOlogist Mazzola and once by a friend who is a professional hypnotist. Although these sessions were intended to help him recall memories of possible abduction, none emerged. When I asked why he had not undergone hypnosis with Hopkins, Robbins said that by the time he began to work with him Hopkins's case-load was too heavy. But he expressed the hope that the opportunity would present itself "to see if there's more that can be brought out, or something that the mind is now ready to reveal that it was not earlier."

During our second conversation, I said to Robbins: "I would like to pose a hypothetical question to you. Imagine that Budd Hopkins, a man for whom you have great respect, were to be elected president in 1988. And imagine that he were to call in top government officials and say, 'I demand to know what the government knows about UFOs.' And imagine they told him, 'President Hopkins, we have told [the public] everything we know. We have no evidence that we have extraterrestrial visitors.' Now, Peter, imagine that President Budd Hopkins called you down to the White House and said: 'I was wrong. There aren't any ET visitors. I don't know what it was that you saw [when you were 14] but there aren't any ET craft in our skies.' Now, Peter, my question to you is, what would be your reaction? Would you be disappointed or relieved?"

Robbins replied, "Neither. I would simply feel that whoever was President had allowed himself to be misled." When I asked if he would suspect that Hopkins would lie to him about such a matter, Robbins replied, "Well, Presidents lie." When I noted that Hopkins was a trusted friend, Robbins responded, "Somebody I trust in the role of a civilian. But in the role of President, people change." Clearly, Robbins has a very deep psychological need to believe in UFOs.

A significantly different account was offered by Robbins's sister Helen, a rock singer, to *New York Times* reporter William E. Geist, according to his article in the July 8, 1987, edition. Geist wrote that Robbins's sister "said she and her brother were [both] abducted when they were children from their front porch in Rockville Centre, New York, by a huge spaceship in broad daylight." Geist quoted her as saying, "The aliens keep taking me for medical tests."

Geist's article also quoted Rosemary Osnato, one of the MUFON panelists, as saying: "When I say I was abducted, a lot of people envy me. Some of them treat me like a saint. I tell them it was horrible and frightening and they don't want to hear it."

Geist's article, describing Hopkins's monthly meetings for "abductees," quoted him as saying: "We serve supper at the meetings and there is a lot of social chatter. If you walked in you would think you were at any other New York cocktail party."

For me, the high point of the MUFON symposium came when Kathie Davis, whom Hopkins considers to be the most impressive "abductee" he has investigated, responded to the question of how the experience had affected her life. Speaking in a soft voice, she responded by saying, "I'm not a speaker and I'm shaking like a leaf." Then came the blockbuster: "I can live with it because I don't believe it. I *really* don't. There's got to be something else"—another explanation.

Her candid statement reminded me of what Hopkins had written in his book: "Kathie nearly always chooses to refer to her UFO experiences as dreams. It is a useful, agreed-upon fiction that I wholeheartedly support." This is a curious twist on the earlier-related joke about the Rorschach test in which it is the therapist (Hopkins) who believes the inkblots are really pornographic pictures.

By the time the abductee session was over, it was almost midnight and I felt it would be an imposition to try to question Kathie Davis at that late hour. I hoped I might see her the next day, but that hope was not realized. Several days later, I wrote to Hopkins asking if he would supply me with Kathie Davis's telephone number so that I might interview her. I promised to make a tape-recording of the interview and to supply copies both to her and to Hopkins. He never responded to my request.

I'm not really surprised, because Kathie has proved to be a

remarkably candid young woman. When she was interviewed by Chicago's WLS-TV for its "Abducted by Aliens" program, she offered the following comment about the dead-grass area in her backyard, which Hopkins had found so very impressive: "My nephew came over and he went out back there and he said to my mother, 'What's wrong with your yard?' That's when we finally went out there and looked and saw it and it was bare. It was just the way it is now. My mom laughed and she said: 'Well, that's where our UFO landed.' "

Possibly it was this off-hand joking comment that inspired Kathie to send photos of the dead-grass area to Budd Hopkins, perhaps as a practical joke or in the hope it might enliven her then drab life. Because of the close friendship that has since developed between them it is doubtful that Kathie's original motivation can ever be known with certainty.

But surely she could never have foreseen that her letter would make her a UFO celebrity, albeit under a pseudonym, and provide the cornerstone for Hopkins's extraterrestrial genetic-experiment theory

Eighteen

Prosaic Alternative

Budd Hopkins, in a paper presented at the 1985 MUFON conference, said: "[I have] spent more time exploring the possibility of a psychological explanation for abduction accounts, have consulted more psychiatrists and psychologists on the subject, and involved a wider array of these professionals in actual investigations than most researchers." Considering that there now are only a handful of people engaged in UFO-abduction research, this claim probably is correct. But when Hopkins went on to claim that *"no psychological explanation, even tentatively, has resulted,"* this raises questions about his choice of consultants and his willingness to consider prosaic explanations.

For example, on April 16, 1987, Hopkins appeared on a popular radio talk-show, "Extension 720," over station WGN in Chicago, hosted by Dr. Milton Rosenberg, professor of psychology at the University of Chicago. Other guests included Dr. Charles L. Gruder, chairman of the psychology department at the University of Illinois at Chicago, and Dr. Martin T. Orne, professor of psychiatry and psychology at the University of Pennsylvania and widely recognized expert on the use of hypnosis. (See Chapter 6.) Orne participated over the telephone from Philadelphia.

Early in the program, Hopkins claimed that, while any single abduction case might seem difficult to accept as fact, the pattern of similarity in many such cases gives them a collective credibility. Gruder challenged this claim by citing an experiment he had himself conducted in which he asked a number of students "to draw a UFO and draw an alien." "I didn't tell them why," he said. When he examined their drawings, Gruder said, "it was surprising that many were quite similar to the drawings" in Hopkins's book.

Hopkins responded, "I don't think that's surprising at all," although in his book he claims such similarities are impressive evidence to support tales of abduction.

Gruder continued: "It isn't surprising because how do people know what a UFO would look like? They read the same stories, the same magazines, [watch] the same science fiction movies. . . ." He noted that Hopkins "mentioned a particular shape of a head, or the fact that the mouth was a line, and I found that most of those [student drawings] were humanoids. Of the 23 [drawings], 18 were human-like. Of these, one-third had big heads, one-third had a line for a mouth, and I figured out that most people who are not artists like yourself don't know how to draw a mouth so they draw a line."

Gruder conceded that "none looked exactly like the picture in [Hopkins's] book, but there were many similarities. The same with the [drawings of] UFOs."

This prompted Hopkins to acknowledge that the Steven Spielberg movie *Close Encounters of the Third Kind,* which was seen by many millions of people, had served to establish the glowing, saucer-shaped craft as the traditional configuration.

Commenting on Hopkins's use of regressive hypnosis, Gruder noted that "hypnosis appears . . . to increase the number of recollections that people report . . . [but] the subject is less able to distinguish accurate from the inaccurate . . . than if they were not hypnotized."

Hopkins responded that in 14 of his abduction cases, or about

10 percent of the total, "recollections were very, very complete . . . without hypnosis." But he added: "I don't think hypnotic recollection is very different than normal non-hypnotic recollection—which is not necessarily valid either."

Milton Rosenberg, noting that UFOs have become "a pervasive modern myth which has been much propagandized, much circulated," also suggested that the general similarity in abduction stories may simply be the result of persons drawing on what they have read about UFOs and seen in movies. Gruder observed that "the people that you [Hopkins] have attracted and have focused on are people who are tending to confirm your hypothesis" because they were sufficiently interested in UFO-abductions to read his book and/or to contact him.

Gruder commented, "A traditional Freudian or other traditional psychoanalyst would have a field day with your [UFOnaut] medical examinations, because they are blatantly sexual; they're rife with symbolism. I couldn't imagine a more perfect symbolic story than a long tube with a small pellet on the end being inserted into someone's nose. . . . Wilhelm Fliess, a colleague of Freud's, believed the nose was the true erogenous zone."

When Martin Orne joined the discussion, he recalled that, when Freud first used hypnosis to treat patients suffering from hysteria, the famous psychiatrist believed that their very detailed recollections, such as a person's facial expression or a torn tapestry, were fact. Later he recognized that such recollections were "mixtures of memories, of fears, of fantasies, of hopes, all kinds of things mixed up," Orne said.

When Rosenberg raised the possibility that the telling of a UFO-abduction story might serve to resolve "some deeper conflict" to fill a subject's psychological need, Orne responded: "Well, there are a lot of secondary gains associated with that. For one thing, you've become the object of interest of a significant person . . . and [the investigator] will spend hours and hours with you. . . . He is fascinated by it and we all love an audience . . . a fascinated audience and [the subject] becomes the center of attention. . . . They suddenly become a celebrity." [Recall that Dr. Slater found that *all* of the Hopkins subjects she tested exhibited low self-esteem.]

When Hopkins challenged Orne's statement on the grounds that three of his 135 subjects (about 3 percent) would never allow their names to be used, Orne responded: "They are celebrities *vis-à-vis* somebody else," that is, in the eyes of Hopkins, other abductionists, and many UFOlogists.

Orne, drawing on his extensive experience in the use of hypnosis, explained how Hopkins's own UFO-abduction expectations can influence his subjects—an effect that Orne calls "demand characteristics." He explained that these "are the demands which are placed upon an individual when you interrogate him . . . to try to elicit some information." Orne said the subject "will try to speak out what is wanted," that is, to supply the answer he or she believes the hypnotist wants.

Persons who contact Hopkins and volunteer to undergo hypnosis know in advance of his strong convictions about UFO-abductions, and thus they know what sort of stories he would like to hear. Typically the subjects believe they have at some time seen a UFO, prompting them to read about UFOs, possibly including Hopkins's books.

When Hopkins claimed that he had "hundreds and hundreds" of "missing-time" reports, Orne responded: "Once you become identified as the man who looks for strange events, strange events will find you. . . . You're somebody who is an explainer of these events." He added: "If an investigator looks for certain kinds of things, [they are] likely to come up over and over in what he finds. That is why Freud found incest fantasies among all of the patients, because he was doing the questioning all of the time."

As the talk-show approached its end, Rosenberg asked Gruder: "What can we learn from this [Hopkins's] book? If you were to use it in a classroom at the University of Illinois . . . ?" Gruder responded that it would be "an excellent tool to teach scientific methodology, because there are all of the problems involved in doing science, certainly as a social scientist, as a psychologist. All of the issues of observation, measurement, reliability, validity, the problems of conducting experiments that you [Rosenberg] mentioned earlier, and gathering data as you mentioned earlier with Dr. Orne—the main characteristics, experimenter bias, evaluation apprehension, controls. All of these issues are present in the [Hopkins] book and would provide a very compelling example for students."

Rosenberg interjected: "You're a very gentlemanly sort; [what] you really mean but haven't directly said is that this book is a *perfect example of errors in all of those areas.*"

Gruder responded: "Certainly, but Budd recognizes and has admitted he is not a scientist. He doesn't claim to be. What disturbs me . . . is just that the presentation [in the book] is as though it were scientific and in fact it's not."

The office of David Jacobs, a member of the faculty of Temple University in Philadelphia, is not far from that of Martin Orne at the University of Pennsylvania. Yet Jacobs has never consulted with the noted specialist despite the fact that Jacobs is now using a newly acquired technique of hypnosis in his new role as an abductionist.

In Jacobs's presentation at the 1986 MUFON conference, he briefly considered possible prosaic explanations for abductee stories but promptly rejected them. Jacobs concluded his talk by observing: "If the abductee stories are not true and the claimants are neither lying nor pathologically disturbed, . . . psychiatry, psychology and psychoanalysis are revolutionized." The anecdotal data that Jacobs, trained as a historian, believes will revolutionize psychiatry and psychology fails to impress specialists trained in those fields, such as Orne, Rosenberg, and Gruder.

Had Jacobs taken time to consult with Orne, or with experienced psychotherapists like the Nissensons, he would have learned of more prosaic, alternative explanations than those he cited and quickly dismissed in his 1986 talk. Perhaps Jacobs did not want to learn about such alternatives.

Nineteen

Latter-day Sigmund Freuds

On June 25, 1988, Budd Hopkins and his principal protégé, David Jacobs, disclosed a revolutionary new theory to challenge the basic underpinnings of traditional psychotherapy; they called it the "Skeleton Key Effect." Because of its potential impact on traditional psychotherapy, one might have expected Hopkins and Jacobs to present the new concept at a conference sponsored by the American Psychological Association or the American Psychiatric Association. Instead, it was unveiled at a UFO conference in Lincoln, Nebraska, sponsored by MUFON.

Hopkins, ignoring what he had been told on the Milton Rosenberg radio talk-show (Chapter 18), declared that "conventional psychological theory cannot explain UFO-abduction experiences [but] UFO-abduction experiences can explain unconventional psychological behavior."

In Hopkins's first book, published in 1981, he suggested that abductees were ordinary folk who represented a "random cross-section of professions, ages and social backgrounds." But at the 1988 MUFON conference, he admitted that many abductees exhibit what he called "unconventional psychological behavior." Jacobs agreed and said many of his subjects suffer "inexplicable phobias, fears and panic disorders." Jacobs refers to such persons as "Unaware Abductees." He and Hopkins claim that these subjects were abducted by UFOs, typically in early childhood, and recollections of the incident have been erased from their memories by the UFOnauts—until recalled under hypnosis.

For example, Jacobs said, they suffer "strong fears of [being in] the basement, their bedroom or backyard. Riding on escalators or elevators can provoke panic." Jacobs said that subjects often report "out-of-body experiences" (OBEs), in which "they in some way left their body, usually during the night [while] in bed. When they floated out of bed they were often accompanied by someone who they interpret as being a deceased relative or an angel." A few even claim to have experienced "astral travel" to other worlds.

Jacobs said that Unaware Abductees exhibit a fascination with "borderland science." For example, they "become obsessed with UFOs. They read all they can about it, join UFO organizations, subscribe to UFO journals." In searching for answers to their personal problems they "find some satisfaction in the fringe aspects of the popular UFO scene, where they often become contactee followers enamored with the possibilities of psychic phenomena. They might join New Age organizations, attend psychic phenomena seminars, and go to psychic conventions."

Jacobs said that "some Unaware Abductees become attracted to 'Channeling' and might even become channelers themselves. They are convinced that alien visitors exist and can be contacted through channeling. The channeled messages that they receive usually reflect benevolent Space Brothers who give beneficial advice about living together in peace and fellowship. . . ." Jacobs added that some are attracted to more fanatical religious groups, where "their quest is primarily for reinforcement *that they are not mentally ill*." (Emphasis added.)

Jacobs admitted that many of the same symptoms also can be found in people who were not abducted by a UFO. Unfortunately, according to Jacobs, "many well-meaning therapists try to convince the abductee that their problems stem from familial relationships in childhood or that their vivid dreams originate in repressed sexuality or in childhood sexual abuse." Such "standard psychological treatment based on clearing up the symptoms without regard to the root cause of the problems has been relatively ineffective in treating the Post-Abduction Syndrome," Jacobs claimed. "When the abductee says that his problems might have something to do with seeing a strange object in the sky, a 'monster' in his bedroom, or an unexplainable missing time event, the [traditional] psychologist routinely tries to convince him that these are just fantasies and that the abductee's problems are based on other psychological causes."

Because most psychotherapists do not accept the reality of UFO-abductions, according to Jacobs, these people "will sometimes go from one therapist to another seeking relief from mental pressures built up by Post-Abduction Syndrome. But they do not find relief." Their only hope, Jacobs claims, is to seek help from someone who is "familiar with both basic psychological techniques and the abduction phenomenon." Presumably he is referring to himself, trained as a historian, or Hopkins, who was trained as an artist.

After a UFO-abduction therapist like Hopkins or Jacobs has made the subject "aware of the root cause of the disturbance," then he or she can "go to a sympathetic professional therapist and find help with traditional therapy," Jacobs said. By "sympathetic professional therapist," Jacobs presumably means one who believes UFOnauts are abducting people as part of an extraterrestrial genetic experiment!

Hopkins provided several specific examples of the sort of counseling he provides his subjects. One involved a man named "Sam," who told Hopkins that as a very young child he had developed a "terror of spiders, particularly Black Widows." So he would seek out spiders under the porch and in other dark places and kill them.

One night, Sam said, he awakened from sleep and thought he saw a nest of spiders on the window, near his face. The next morning he said he had "begged my mother to kill the spiders and take away

their nest." But, curiously, "there wasn't any nest . . . and no spiders."
The child's mother concluded that he had simply *dreamed* about
spiders on the window.

But Hopkins rejected this prosaic explanation and asked Sam
to try to describe the appearance of the spider nest he recalled seeing
many years earlier. When Sam said it was white, and held up his
two hands to illustrate the appearance of the two spiders, he remarked
that their eyes were "black and shiny." Immediately, Hopkins said,
both he and Sam knew "what the truth was; he had seen a white
face in the corner of the window, a *white alien face* with two black,
shiny, elliptical eyes—the same face he'd described on other
occasions."

Hopkins commented that "the cause of [Sam's] phobia lay revealed. Years and years of spider-dread . . . all caused by what turned
out to be the first stage of a UFO-abduction. *Sam was more amazed
even than I at what the 'skeleton key' had unlocked.*" (Emphasis
added.)

Another of Hopkins's subjects, a woman called "Joan," wrote
to him after reading his book to report that one night she had
awakened to find a strange-looking creature in her room. Later,
prior to undergoing hypnosis by Hopkins, she told him that many
years earlier she had been the victim of incest involving her older
brother and that it had been a devastating experience. When Hopkins
asked Joan if she now had trouble getting along with her brother
and she replied that she liked him, Hopkins said he was "bewildered."
He found it inconceivable that she could forgive her brother, so
Hopkins sought an extraterrestrial explanation.

Under hypnosis, Hopkins reported, that Joan recalled a "classic
UFO abduction incident which had occurred when she was only
four or five years old." Hopkins concluded that "the real childhood
trauma had been her UFO abduction, while the later [incest] incident
with her brother served only to underline [the] abduction's emotional
effect." This, Hopkins observed, explains "why her brother never
became the true target of her anger and fear; he had not been their

original cause."

Another subject, an attractive young woman named Kris Florence (Chapter 17), under hypnosis by Hopkins, recalled that as a child of five or six she had used a stick to uproot an ant-hill. In doing so, she uncovered some large ant eggs, which she said she promptly squashed with a stick. Then she looked around for other ant-hills and repeated the operation.

While many people might find such actions not terribly unusual for a child of that age, Hopkins was mystified. But when Kris said that the ant eggs were "kind of whitish and smooth and shiny" and that her dislike of their appearance persisted, the explanation became obvious to therapist Hopkins. He concluded that the ant eggs re-minded Kris of the UFO creatures who had abducted her shortly before the first ant-hill incident, and she believed that the eggs belonged to the UFOnauts.

(After hearing this account, I was tempted to inform Hopkins that as a young boy in Iowa I was fascinated to watch the transition of tadpoles into frogs. But I feared that if Hopkins asked me to describe the eyes of the tadpoles—which were black, shiny, and slanted—he would conclude that I had been the victim of UFO-abduction in my childhood.)

Jacobs provided his MUFON audience with a titillating account of Unaware Abductees he has treated. He reported that "a young girl or boy may be abducted numerous times from the time they are five years old. Typically . . . they are stripped naked. . . . Every inch of their bodies is examined and touched. Their genitals are probed and manipulated. . . . By the time a female abductee has reached 16 years of age she might already have had a number of traumatic internal examinations. . . ."

"To complicate matters," Jacobs said, "while the Aliens are per-forming their procedures on them, young boys and girls can sometimes look over to other tables . . . to see naked adults being examined and probed. Girls stare in shock as the Aliens perform procedures on the man's sometimes erect genitals. When the Alien is finished with a young girl, he simply turns around and walks out of the room while she is laying [*sic*] there with the residue of sensuous feeling.

"In other less frequent scenarios, the Aliens might even urge the girl who is going through puberty to 'breed' now that she can bear children. They might conjure up mental 'pictures' in an 11-year-old girl's mind of humans having sexual intercourse or they might flood her mind with clinical images of the physical details of intercourse to instruct her," Jacobs said.

The new "Skeleton Key Effect" even provides an explanation for the genesis of homosexuality, according to Jacobs: "If a 'female' [Alien] performs the procedures enough times, then women abductees might develop a sexual preference for women rather than men." The new theory may also explain nymphomania, according to Jacobs. "One abductee said that she went from man to man trying to recapture the feeling [of intercourse with a UFOnaut] but was never able to duplicate it. . . ."

It will be recalled that subjects under hypnosis are inclined to tell a hypnotist what they think he wants to hear, and that the abduction tales reported to Leo Sprinkle are much more benevolent than those told to Hopkins (Chapter 16). It is interesting that Jacobs reports far more lurid sexual encounters than either Hopkins or Sprinkle.

Jacobs admits that some of the subjects he and Hopkins counsel *"think that they are mentally unbalanced. . . . The problems can be so extremely severe that thoughts of suicide are not rare for adults and even young children."* (Emphasis added.)

In an interview published in the Spring 1988 issue of *UFO* magazine, Hopkins said: "In the past year, I've had to deal, directly or indirectly, with at least two children who have tried to take their own lives. And I've dealt with one man whose father *did* commit suicide. It seems to be very much connected with his reading my book and *Communion* and getting terrified all over again."

If a psychologically disturbed person seeks counsel from a

traditional psychotherapist who concludes that the patient's problems arise, for example, because of an unhappy childhood due to an alcoholic mother or father, there is some hope for the patient's recovery. But if a psychologically disturbed person seeks counsel from Hopkins or Jacobs, they are likely to conclude that they were abducted by UFOnauts to participate in an extraterrestrial genetic experiment from which there is no hope of escape. They believe that they possibly will undergo that experience again and, worse yet, that their children and their grandchildren are doomed to undergo the same hideous experience. It is hardly surprising that this prospect prompts consideration of suicide. I will be surprised if there are not more such tragedies in the coming years.

Twenty

Fantasy-prone Persons

Budd Hopkins claims that he probably has expended as much energy in the search for prosaic psychological explanations for UFO-abduction accounts as anyone. He admits that "individual accounts here and there may indeed have conventional psychological causes," i.e., explanations. But Hopkins claims that "no [single] blanket explanation for the mass of similar reports—not even a tentative psychological theory—has ever been presented to me by first-hand investigators."

This is hardly surprising inasmuch as there is "no [single] blanket explanation" for *all* reports of human illness, nor a single explanation for why some people commit crimes, or a single explanation for why television sets malfunction. Hopkins further qualifies his claim by limiting his sources to those he feels give sufficient credibility to the idea of UFO-abductions to become "first-hand investigators."

That the reports are slightly similar in a few respects is not surprising in view of the tens of millions in the United States and Canada who have been exposed to UFO-abduction films, television shows, books by Strieber and Hopkins, and their extensive appearances on radio and television talk-shows.

Dr. Robert A. Baker, a seasoned professor of psychology at the University of Kentucky, offered a number of well-established prosaic explanations for UFO-abduction tales in a paper published in the Winter 1987-88 issue of CSICOP's *Skeptical Inquirer.* Dr. Baker noted that many UFO-abductions reportedly occur after a person has gone to bed, suggesting a phenomenon known to psychologists as hypnogogic hallucinations—if experienced when falling asleep —or hypnopompic hallucinations, if experienced while awakening.

One of the characteristics of such hallucinations is that they seem very real. Another is that the subject feels paralyzed, or seems to be floating outside his or her body, as many "UFO-abductees" report. Typically, after the hallucination, the subject falls asleep. Baker emphasized that "ordinary, perfectly sane and rational people have these hallucinatory experiences and that such individuals are in no way mentally disturbed or psychotic."

Confirmation of Baker's statement came in a number of letters submitted to the *Skeptical Inquirer* by its readers. One, published in the Summer 1988 issue, began: "I would like to thank Robert A. Baker for his article. . . . I have been plagued by hypnogogic hallucinations since childhood, but until reading his article I didn't know what they were called or even that other people had them." The letter described a typical hypnogogic hallucination: "Though I seem awake, my body is completely paralyzed. I feel my 'spirit' leave my body. . . . Sometimes I float all around the house, and on one occasion I floated through a wall and out into the yard. . . . Over the years I have seen and talked to 'ghosts,' been visited (though not yet abducted) by aliens. . . . These experiences seem as real as life." (Almost certainly Hopkins and Jacobs would conclude that they were actual occurrences.)

Another reader described a hypnopompic hallucination that he said "still seems as real to me as any of my experiences in a waking state. . . . I had never heard of such a thing before reading this article."

Commenting on the use of hypnosis to try to probe for hidden memories of UFO-abduction, Baker cited an article coauthored by two psychologists: Dr. Sheryl C. Wilson and Dr. T. X. Barber— a leading authority on the use of hypnosis. In the article, Barber and Wilson wrote: "Although this study provided a broader under-standing of the kind of life experiences that may underlie the ability to be an excellent hypnotic subject, it has also led to a serendipitous finding that has wide implication for all of psychology—*it has shown that there exists a small group of individuals (possibly four percent of the population) who fantasize a large part of the time, who typically 'see,' 'hear,' 'smell,' and 'touch' and fully experience what they fantasize; and who can be labeled fantasy-prone individuals.*" (Emphasis added.)

When such fantasy-prone individuals were given hypnotic suggestions, calling for visual and auditory hallucinations, they re-sponded readily. Barber and Wilson concluded that "we are asking them to do for us the kind of thing they can do independently of us in their daily lives."

Baker observed that such persons typically "have learned to be highly secretive and private about their fantasy lives." However, when such fantasy-prone persons undergo hypnosis by UFO-abductionists like Hopkins and Jacobs, "it provides them with a social situation in which they are encouraged to do, and are rewarded for doing, what *they usually do only in secrecy and in private.*" (Emphasis added.)

Instead of feeling guilty for being a day-dreamer, a fantasy-prone person who tells a tale of UFO-abduction (after acquiring a few details from a book by Hopkins or Strieber) can quickly become a celebrity by appearing on radio and television talk-shows. At the very least they can believe that they are so genetically superior that they have been selected for an extraterrestrial breeding experiment—before they realize the long-term consequences of such belief.

When Baker spoke at the 1988 CSICOP conference in Chicago, on November 5, he described the results of an experiment he had earlier conducted using several hundred "very, very normal, sane, run-of-the-mill" volunteers whom he hypnotically regressed to a "previous life." Approximately a hundred of the subjects also were projected via hypnosis into the future, to describe their lives. "Some of these past and future lives were quite dramatic, while others were dull and prosaic," Baker reported, "depending upon the personality of the subject, his/her interest in science-fiction, and whether or not he/she was a fantasy-prone personality type."

"Two of my fantasy-prone types, for example, would win Academy Awards (for their acting ability)," Baker said. One man was regressed weekly for a year with a different role each week—ranging from a Roman soldier to a London prostitute. Baker reported that this subject's "role-play during each of these fantasies was highly vivid and dramatic, and included moans, groans, shrieks, tears, very feminine voices, screams of agony, rage, and soaking perspiration."

Another fantasy-prone subject, a woman, when given the hypnotic suggestion that she was being taken into the future, "became a bar-girl and torch-singer in the largest human colony on Mars in the twenty-second century," Baker said. He added: "Her description of the colony and her songs, complete with words and music, were truly astonishing."

Baker cited the results of a survey conducted a century ago and published by Edmund Parish in 1894, entitled "Nature and Frequency of the Occurrence of Hallucinations in the Sane." For the survey, ordinary people living in the United States, England, France, Germany, and the Netherlands were asked: "Have you ever, when believing yourself to be completely awake, had a vivid impression of seeing or being touched by a living being or inanimate object, or of hearing a voice; which impression, so far as you could discover, was not due to any external physical cause?"

Of the 27,329 persons surveyed, *nearly 12 percent answered "yes,"* Baker reported. "Although a certain proportion [of these] could be explained away—most could not and follow-up investigations of a number of the individual cases clearly showed the validity of 'waking hallucinations' and established the fact that they are much more common than one would suspect."

If even a small percent of the U.S. population experiences occasional daytime hallucinations, and if 4 percent is fantasy-prone, as Barber and Wilson's data indicate, it is not surprising that Hopkins and Jacobs are able to "discover" hundreds of people who can spin UFO-abduction tales that these abductionists find credible, especially since Hopkins and Jacobs are so eager to believe in UFO-abductions.

Baker also cited a phenomenon well known to psychologists, called "folie a deux," in which one of two closely associated people develops certain mental symptoms, particularly delusions, which are communicated to and accepted by the other person. The person suffering from the delusion is the dominant individual, while the one who develops the induced delusion is the more submissive and suggestible. During hypnosis of suspected UFO-abductees, Hopkins or Jacobs typically functions as the hypnotist who plays a dominant role in the procedure while the subject is in an especially suggestible state of mind. This prompted Baker to suggest that "the dominant individual suffering from the delusion is Hopkins or Jacobs—not the alleged abductee."

The foregoing provides a useful perspective on Hopkins's repeated claim that he has searched in vain for possible prosaic psychological explanations for the fanciful tales of UFO-abduction.

Twenty-one

UFOlogy's Pariah—or Messiah?

Whitley Strieber, who once aspired to be the messiah for the UFO movement, has become its pariah, despite the massive publicity that UFOlogists enjoyed because of *Communion*. His new UFO-abduction book, *Transformation,* published in the fall of 1988, will not enhance his standing.

The rejection of Strieber by many UFOlogists stems in part from his increasingly bad relations with Budd Hopkins, who is the UFO movement's acknowledged "abduction-guru" (Chapter 14). In 1988, MUFON's members selected Hopkins as the person who had made the greatest contribution to UFOlogy during the previous year the second time he has received this award.

Strieber is a pariah also because even those credulous UFOlogists who accept UFO-abductions as fact find Strieber's tales too bizarre to believe. Behind the scenes, Hopkins has been critical of his now famous subject and rival. For example, in June of 1987, when *Communion* was leading the best-seller lists while Hopkins's *Intruders* lagged far behind, Hopkins privately circulated a "White Paper" among leaders of the UFO movement. It denied a published claim that Hopkins believed Strieber to be "a sane, trustworthy and stable individual." This White Paper revealed other bizarre Strieber tales that, according to Hopkins, had been proved false. For example, Hopkins said that when he asked Strieber why he had guns and elaborate security systems at his remote cabin, Strieber explained that "a right-wing southern group" had made death threats against him and had threatened to kidnap his son. In a subsequent conversation, Strieber admitted that there had been no such threats, Hopkins said.

Since Strieber was anxious to meet "Kathie Davis" (Chapter 9), Hopkins said, he arranged for them to meet for lunch during one of her visits to New York. During their conversation, according to Hopkins, Strieber said: "I think I've seen you before, Kathie, inside a UFO. But it wasn't *all* of you. *It was just your head, and it was alive, and it was on a shelf."* (Emphasis added.)

Hopkins characterized Strieber's account as presented in *Communion* as "one of the most confused and least reliable currently in print." But, Hopkins said, "I firmly believe [Strieber] is an abductee."

Strieber, stung by the negative reaction of many UFOlogists to *Communion,* publicly admitted that "there is a terrific strain in my relationship with the UFO community" in an article published in the June 1988 *MUFON UFO Journal.* Strieber claimed his book had done "more for the cause of the UFO community than anything that has happened in the past quarter century." He charged that "too many UFO researchers believe the Budd Hopkins 'abduction scenario,' assuming it to be holy writ. . . . I have received literally thousands of narratives from people who have never been hypnotized and never been near a UFO researcher. If even a small percentage of their stories are true, then the Hopkins scenario cannot be the whole answer."

Strieber criticized "a large number of researchers out there hypnotizing people . . . (who) have no mental health credentials. . . . I believe that much 'abduction research' is actually unintentional brainwashing. . . . Its effect is to leave already troubled people in much worse shape. I feel that it's only a matter of time before somebody is hurt, either driven psychotic or to suicide. . . ." This criticism echoed my own, expressed in the hard-cover edition of this book which Strieber had read.

Similar criticism, not likely to endear Strieber to Hopkins's many supporters in the UFO movement, appears in the closing pages of Strieber's new book: "I have withdrawn from contact with UFO researchers who have no professional credentials and seem to mix fear and ignorance in equal amounts. Many of these people are hypnotizing distraught human beings, in effect operating as untrained and unlicensed counselors and therapists, and innocently imposing their own beliefs on their victims."

In *Communion*, Strieber claimed that the UFOnauts spoke to him sometimes in an accent he characterized as "startlingly Midwestern." In *Transformation*, Strieber reports that he now hears voices *when no one else is present*. On one occasion, when Strieber was enjoying an ice cream cone, he reports hearing a voice cry out: "Can you stop eating that?" (Earlier, Strieber reported that a female UFOnaut had warned him: "If you continue to eat sweets, you cannot hope to live long, and if you eat chocolate you will die.") At other times the voices that Strieber reports hearing offer a much more profound message. For example: "This is the field where the sins of the world are buried."

Strieber admits that claims of hearing "disembodied voices" are "a classic symptom of schizophrenia." Also, that persons suffering paranoia "hear voices, and often these voices give them commands." Elsewhere in the book Strieber tells of voices that instruct him: "Go to the middle of the meadow and look up," or "Don't scream or you'll wake up Andrew" (his young son).

But Strieber dismisses any possibility that mental illness might explain the voices he hears because "there was something very ordinary about these voices. They sounded like people, and they weren't commanding me in grandiloquent terms." More important, according to Strieber, "was the total absence of other symptoms that would be associated with psychological disease." Strieber fails to inform readers of *Transformation* that his psychiatrist, Dr. Donald Klein, had written him on July 26, 1986, saying that his symptoms suggested the possibility of temporal lobe epilepsy (Chapter 13).

At the end of *Transformation,* in Appendix 1, Strieber briefly discusses the question of whether his bizarre tales might be the result of mental illness. Strieber writes: "There are a number of diseases of the brain and disorders of the mind that can lead to hallucinations. The most prominent disease is temporal lobe epilepsy [TLE], which is a transient disturbance of the temporal lobe of the brain. It causes vivid hallucinations that are often associated with powerful odors [which Strieber reports during some of his UFOnaut encounters]. Less frequently, *sounds* can be mixed with visions and smells in this disease. People with temporal lobe epilepsy tend to be verbal and philosophical and to lack a sense of humor." (Emphasis added.)

Strieber reports in *Transformation* that he "was tested for temporal lobe epilepsy on December 6, *1986,* and no abnormalities were found." Strieber acknowledges that because of the transient nature of TLE, he has "continued to have myself tested for it. I undertook another test series beginning on March 14, *1988.*"

This conflicts with what Strieber earlier wrote in *Communion,* and what he later wrote me, as recounted in Chapter 13. At the time Strieber now says he took his *first* TLE test, on December 6, 1986, *Communion* must certainly have been in the process of printing, because it was in bookstores by late January 1987. Yet in *Communion* (p. 130), Strieber claimed he had undergone tests by *two* neurologists who reported "absolutely normal temporal lobe function." But several months *after* his book was out, Strieber wrote me, on May 3, 1987, to say that one of the neurologists had not completed his investigation.

Now, in *Transformation,* Strieber offers still another account which claims he took one TLE test on December 6, 1986, and another beginning March 14, *1988*—more than a year after *Communion* was published. Strieber claims that the 1988 tests, which included brain scans using CAT (computer axial tomography) and MRI (magnetic resonance imaging), "would have located epileptic areas in the brain of an adult with longstanding (two years or more) disease. No such areas were observed," according to Strieber.

However, Strieber reports that the MRI scan did reveal several "unknown bright objects" in his brain. But he quotes his neurologist as saying that these are "occasionally seen with this test in normal brains."

Strieber writes: "*Most* of the physicians involved in my case have requested confidentiality." (Emphasis added.) For this reason, Strieber said, he will not release the names of *any* of his physicians— even those who did not request anonymity.

Strieber said he has turned over all of the medical findings to his close personal friend Dr. John Gliedman, a psychologist, and that Gliedman "has agreed to correspond with licensed medical and mental-health professionals and concerned scientists about my case. We will not respond to 'investigators' without scientific, medical, or mental-health credentials, or to 'debunkers' intent on twisting the facts to serve their own emotional needs, and not to get at the truth." At least several professional psychologists who meet Strieber's stated requirements have written to Gliedman but as of this writing they have not received any response.

In *Transformation,* Strieber reports he was abducted again on December 23, 1986—shortly before *Communion* was published. He found himself standing in "an ordinary room . . . in front of a big, plainly designed desk. Behind it was a wall of bookcases stacked with books. There was a volume of Bruce Catton's work on the Civil War . . . a number of vaguely familiar novels of forties and fifties vintage, a volume of Kafka, some books on mathematics, and, pulled partway out of a shelf as if to draw attention to it, Thomas Wolfe's *You Can't Go Home Again.*"

Whereas UFOnauts traditionally are said to be quite short, Strieber reports seeing "a tall man in a tan jumpsuit . . . easily six feet six." Sitting behind the desk, according to Strieber, was "what looked to me like a man . . . [with] a ridiculous excuse for a curly black toupee on his head." Strieber also reported seeing "a woman . . . wearing a blue jumpsuit. . . . Her hair was brown and pulled back into a bun behind her head."

In Strieber's new book he reports several OBEs. In one instance, he reports awakening and seeing a creature he described as resembling a giant, ugly insect. Although the giant insect glared at Strieber, he said "there was also the love. I felt mothered. Caressed." Then Strieber claims he was transported to another place where he saw "a perfectly ordinary-looking human being. . . . He was naked." Suddenly a tall person, dressed in black, began "beating the poor . . . [naked] man with a terrible whip. . . . This man was almost torn to pieces by the fury of the beating." Strieber says that a voice informed him that the man was being punished because "he failed to get you [Strieber] to obey him."

On another occasion, in late 1986, Strieber heard voices say: "Oh, good. Now we'll show you something." "An instant later," he writes, "I appeared to be in two places at once. I was still lying on the bed, but a quite conscious and sensually alive 'other' me was also standing beside what was clearly a new Cadillac."

Perhaps the most incredible tale in *Transformation* reportedly occurred in late January 1987, shortly after *Communion* was published. According to Strieber, Bruce Lee, a senior editor with Strieber's publisher, and his wife were browsing in a bookstore on Manhattan's upper east side when "he noticed two people enter the store and move without hesitation directly to the display of *Communion*." Reportedly, Lee moved closer to the couple and noted they "were both short, perhaps five feet tall, and were wearing scarves pulled up to cover their chins, large dark glasses, and winter hats pulled low over their foreheads."

According to Strieber, the couple were scanning very rapidly through *Communion*, making comments such as "Oh, he's got that wrong!" and "It wasn't like that." Lee reportedly approached the couple to ask what they found wrong, but they did not respond. When Lee "noticed that behind their dark glasses, both the man and woman had large, black, almond-shaped eyes"—suggesting they were extraterrestrials—Lee and his wife quickly departed without waiting to see if the mysterious couple bought a copy of the book.

In Appendix 2 of *Transformation,* Strieber quotes from a letter I wrote to him on December 17, 1987, in which I expressed the view that he "honestly believes he experienced the weird encounters described in his book *Communion* and that he is not knowingly, intentionally, falsifying same." Strieber added that I suspect he is suffering temporal lobe epilepsy. He rejected this on the grounds that "no evidence of this disease—or any other intrusive abnormality—has been found, even with extensive testing."

We must take this Strieber claim on faith—knowing that in *Communion* he cited a number of instances of tales he had repeatedly told that he now admits are not true. In my correspondence with Strieber, even on rather mundane matters, I found he has great difficulty in "keeping his story straight."

Transformation provides still more such evidence. For example, Strieber claims (p. 27) that he and his wife had a firm policy of keeping their son Andrew "*strictly isolated* from talk about [UFO] visitors." (Emphasis added.) Only seven pages earlier, Strieber wrote that Andrew had "been told little about the visitors." Later, p. 211, Strieber reports that when Andrew awakened one morning he "was full of questions about the visitors. . . . We never discuss them with him unless he brings them up. . . ." But when Strieber appeared at the 1987 MUFON conference symposium on UFO-abductions (Chapter 17), his young son was in attendance. Whitley introduced me to him after the lengthy abduction sessions were completed.

Strieber is likely to remain a pariah in the UFO movement because of his ambivalence about whether his bizarre experiences are due to extraterrestrial visitors. In Strieber's *MUFON UFO Journal* article, he criticized an interview published in *Twilight Zone* magazine that quoted him as saying, "I don't necessarily think I was abducted aboard a spacecraft by extraterrestrials." He charged the article was flawed because it omitted his comment "but I'd be very surprised if I wasn't." Only a couple of months before this article appeared Strieber was interviewed on the "Larry King Live" television show and was asked about being abducted by extraterrestrials. He replied: "In *Communion,* I do not say that I was abducted by alien visitors from another planet."

In *Transformation,* Strieber cites two polygraph tests he has taken. Questions included in the tests were: "Are the visitors about whom you write in your book *Communion* a physical reality?" and "Do you honestly believe that the visitors are physically real?" Strieber answered yes to both questions and the polygraph examiner concluded he was being truthful. Yet in the introduction to Strieber's new book he writes: "I do not think we are dealing with something as straightforward as the arrival of a scientific team from another planet that is here to study us."

In the closing pages of *Transformation,* Strieber tries to clarify this ambivalence in the following words: "The visitors are physically real. They also function on a nonphysical level, and this may be their primary reality."

Twenty-two

The "Hopkins Syndrome"

In advancing the hypothesis that UFO-abductions are part of an extraterrestrial genetic experiment, Hopkins and Jacobs overlook the most mystifying aspect of their bizarre theory: Why have the ETs focused almost exclusively on citizens of the United States?

According to BUFORA's Jenny Randles, only a tiny handful of claimed abductees had surfaced in Britain as of mid-1987—prior to Whitley Strieber's visit there to promote his first UFO-abduction book. I am aware of only a single abduction case in France, and the young man subsequently confessed it was a hoax. To my knowledge, there are no UFO-abduction reports from Switzerland or West Germany, nor from the Soviet Union or the Peoples' Republic of China—both of whose populations are larger than that of the United States.

A possible explanation for this curious situation is that the UFOnauts find U.S. citizens to be vastly superior genetically to those of other countries. The more logical explanation is that the growing fantasy of UFO-abductions has been sparked by the widespread news media coverage in the United States of the Hopkins and Strieber books. The fantasy has been widely promoted here, especially by many television and radio talk-shows which do not hesitate to use sensationalism to attract a larger audience, thereby enhancing their "ratings" and their profits. In most other countries, radio and television are government-operated monopolies that do not face such competitive pressures.

In the United States, television shows on the subject, seen by millions, usually offer viewers an extremely biased treatment. For example, during the Oprah Winfrey show (Chapter 12) I was the only skeptic appearing with Hopkins and four women who claimed to be abductees. During the one-hour program, I was "on-camera" for a total of less than five minutes. During ABC's popular "20/20" network-TV show on May 14, 1987, one segment focused on Hopkins and several of his subjects. The lone skeptic, a psychologist, was given barely one minute to respond to more than ten minutes of abduction fantasy. During a 20-minute segment of the CBS "Nightwatch" television talk-show in the spring of 1987, dealing with UFO-abductions, the only guests were Hopkins and one of his subjects, Michael Shea.

Strieber has repeatedly refused to participate in any talk-show if I am to be present. Shortly after Hopkins and I appeared together on the Oprah Winfrey show, Hopkins announced that henceforth he would not appear on any program on which I was a guest. By this means, Hopkins and Strieber minimize the possibility that they will be challenged by a knowledgeable skeptic. As a result, the public is denied the opportunity to hear both sides of the controversy. It is shocking that talk-show hosts will allow a guest to dictate who can appear on their programs. But many are willing to accept such censorship to boost their ratings.

The UFO myth itself, which started more than 40 years ago in the United States, has swept the world, generating reports from the remotest parts of the globe. If and when foreign-language editions of the Strieber and Hopkins books are published, I predict there will be similar UFO-abduction reports from other countries.

This already has occurred in Canada, where the public is exposed to many of the same books and radio and television programs broadcast in the United States. South America should soon follow. It has long been a source of bizarre UFO tales, including one of the first abduction-rape reports in the early 1960s. It came from a Brazilian peasant who claimed he was forced to make love to a beautiful, voluptuous female captain of a UFO. At the time, this report was dismissed as wild fantasy by most serious UFOlogists.

If the UFO-abduction fantasy spreads around the globe, Hopkins, Jacobs, and other abductionists will have a ready explanation: The UFOnauts have finally decided to sample the ova and sperm of the citizens of other nations. Perhaps one of a handful of Soviet UFOlogists will claim to have discovered an abductee—proving that Communist ova and sperm are up to ET requirements.

When the U.S. news media tire of giving space and air-time to abduction-claimants, as eventually will occur, I predict that the number of new abduction-claimants will taper off. Abductionists will have a ready explanation: The UFOnauts now have enough ova, sperm, and flesh samples to meet the needs of their genetic experiment. To spark lagging news media interest, a new type of abductee may emerge—the "transportees." They will describe visits to the UFOnauts' homeland, where there is no poverty, no illness, no illicit drug problem, and no war.

The abductionists will continue to enjoy their "game," but for some victims it will have proved to be a dangerous one. They will carry the resulting mental scars to their graves, and some of these will be passed along to their children. How tragic! How unnecessary!

It is hoped that some victims will turn to qualified psychotherapists. When this occurs, I suggest that their malaise be called the "Hopkins Syndrome." While Hopkins was not the first to discover "covert UFO-abductions," in my opinion he has become the "Typhoid Mary" of this tragic malaise. Without realizing it, I believe he has also become one of its victims.

Index